PETER

Opening up 1 Peter

ANDREW THOMSON

DayOne

ALSO BY ANDREW THOMSON ...

Commendations for *Opening up Deuteronomy*:

This commentary ... is perceptive in its comments, lively in style and most helpful in relating the teaching of the book to the overall theology of the Bible. Bible students and preachers will find it stimulating. I will be recommending it warmly.

Allan M. Harman, former Principal and Professor of Old Testament, Presbyterian Theological College, Melbourne, Australia, and author of *Deuteronomy: The Commands of a Covenant God* (Christian Focus, 2001).

Crisp, clear and contemporary. For any who wish to delve into Deuteronomy either as a group or for private study, this is just right.

Brian Edwards, Christian minister, author and editor

If you want a quick path into Old Testament thought, read Deuteronomy; if you want a quick path into Deuteronomy, read *Opening Up Deuteronomy* by Andrew Thomson. There you have in a nutshell the highest commendation and the best advice I can give. Dr Thomson (is he a Dr? If not, he should be!) is blessed with a straightforward and readable prose style. His meaning is never in doubt. He understands and is fair to the covenantal basis and structure of Deuteronomy; he has a rightly Mosaic approach and a covetable understanding of what is happening in each part and at each stage of Moses' book. Deuteronomy is itself an application to the Lord's people, for the purposes of their coming new life in Canaan, of the basic Mosaic revelation, and it has found in Thomson a writer skilled in 'applicatory explanation' whereby, so to speak, we discover in one move what Deuteronomy is about, what individual passages and verses mean, how difficulties are explained and what the whole means for our lives today. This is a book to read with pleasure and profit and to give away with confidence.

Alec Motyer, review in *Evangelicals Now*

First printed 2016

ISBN 978-1-84625-553-3

British Library Cataloguing in Publication Data available

Published by Day One Publications

Ryelands Road, Leominster, England, HR6 8NZ

Telephone 01568 613 740 FAX 01568 611 473

email—sales@dayone.co.uk

web site—www.dayone.co.uk

Printed by TJ International

This book is sent out
to the glory of our faithful Creator,
with the prayer that every reader will be either
helped through present suffering or
better equipped for future suffering.

List of Bible abbreviations

THE OLD TESTAMENT

Gen.	Genesis	1 Chr.	1 Chronicles	Dan.	Daniel
Exod.	Exodus	2 Chr.	2 Chronicles	Hosea	Hosea
Lev.	Leviticus	Ezra	Ezra	Joel	Joel
Num.	Numbers	Neh.	Nehemiah	Amos	Amos
Deut.	Deuteronomy	Esth.	Esther	Obad.	Obadiah
Josh.	Joshua	Job	Job	Jonah	Jonah
Judg.	Judges	Ps.	Psalms	Micah	Micah
Ruth	Ruth	Prov.	Proverbs	Nahum	Nahum
1 Sam.	1 Samuel	Eccles.	Ecclesiastes	Hab.	Habakkuk
2 Sam.	2 Samuel	S.of S.	Song of Solomon	Zeph.	Zephaniah
1 Kings	1 Kings	Isa.	Isaiah	Hag.	Haggai
2 Kings	2 Kings	Jer.	Jeremiah	Zech.	Zechariah
		Lam.	Lamentations	Mal.	Malachi
		Ezek.	Ezekiel		

THE NEW TESTAMENT

Matt.	Matthew	Gal.	Galatians	Heb.	Hebrews
Mark	Mark	Eph.	Ephesians	James	James
Luke	Luke	Phil.	Philippians	1 Peter	1 Peter
John	John	Col.	Colossians	2 Peter	2 Peter
Acts	Acts	1 Thes.	1 Thessalonians	1 John	1 John
Rom.	Romans	2 Thes.	2 Thessalonians	2 John	2 John
1 Cor.	1 Corinthians	1 Tim.	1 Timothy	3 John	3 John
2 Cor.	2 Corinthians	2 Tim.	2 Timothy	Jude	Jude
		Titus	Titus	Rev.	Revelation
		Philem.	Philemon		

Contents

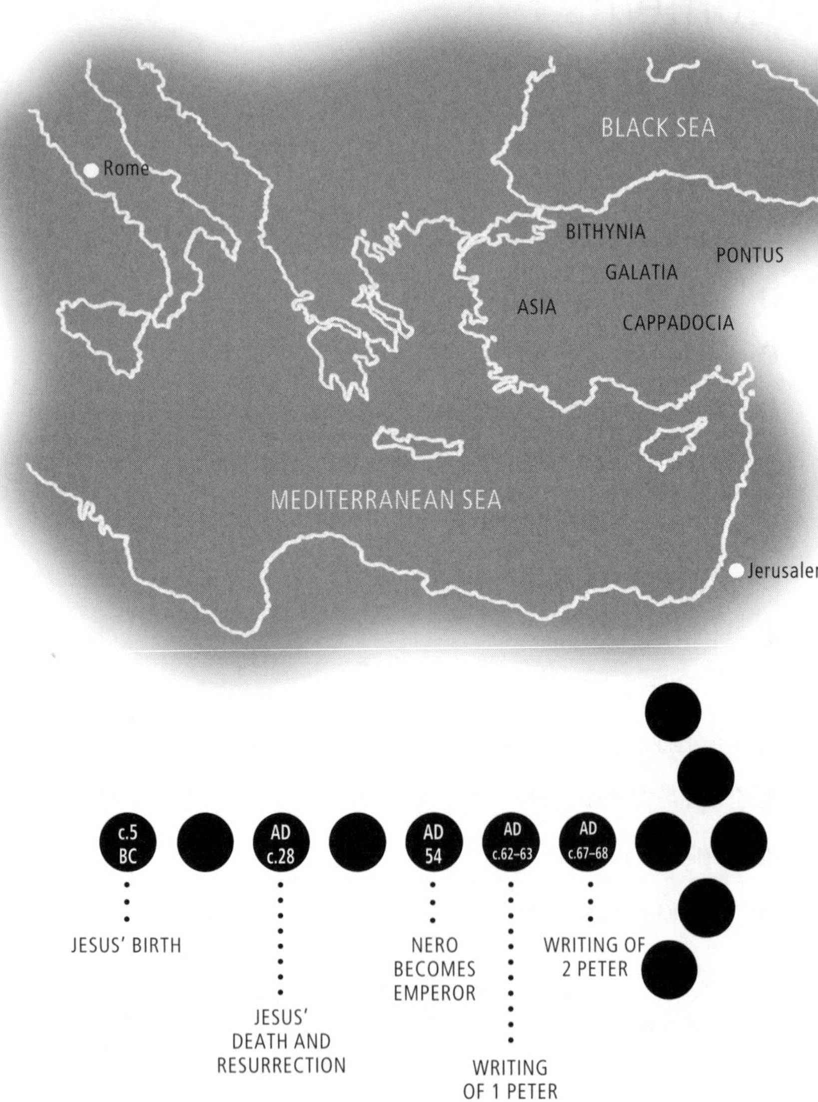
BLACK SEA
Rome
BITHYNIA
PONTUS
GALATIA
ASIA
CAPPADOCIA
MEDITERRANEAN SEA
Jerusalem
c.5 BC
JESUS' BIRTH
AD c.28
JESUS' DEATH AND RESURRECTION
AD 54
NERO BECOMES EMPEROR
AD c.62–63
WRITING OF 1 PETER
AD c.67–68
WRITING OF 2 PETER

Part 1
Introduction

1 Encouragement for exiles

(1:1–2)

We all need help—especially when we're suffering in some way. And that help is appreciated all the more when it comes from someone who knows our weakness. Peter is just the man for the job, and this letter is designed to give us the help we all need.

From ...

From 'Peter' (v. 1)

Peter, the rock. Peter, the first disciple to confess that Jesus was the Christ, the Son of the living God (Matt. 16:16). Peter, the disciple determined not to deny his master, even at the cost of his life (Matt. 26:35). Peter, the only follower ready to defend and protect his Lord as he was arrested. Peter, the first one to go into the empty tomb. Peter, the one who stood and addressed the multitude on the day of Pentecost. Peter, the fisherman who astonished the Jewish council with his boldness, and made it clear (twice!

Acts 4:19; 5:29) that he would follow God's orders rather than theirs. Peter, the first preacher of the gospel to Gentiles.

But this is the same Peter who argued with the Saviour about going to the cross, and spoke on Satan's behalf; the same Peter who had been so confident that he would prove faithful, and yet who was so wrong. It's the same Peter who denied his Lord, not once, but three times, intimidated by a servant girl. It's the same Peter who undermined the gospel by withdrawing from sharing meals with Gentiles in Antioch, because of peer pressure.

It's as if there were two Peters, and that was the problem. It's our problem too. We all have an 'old man' that we need to be 'putting off', and a 'new man' that we need to be 'putting on' (Eph. 4:22–24; Col. 3:9–14). Every Christian has an internal battle and could be described as a 'walking civil war'. As if to highlight this struggle, Simon Peter had two names, one harking back to the fisherman he had been (when he 'heard'—the meaning of the name Simon—Christ's call to follow), the other pointing forward to what Christ was to make him (a reliable witness to his identity, a rock—the meaning of the name Peter—on which to build the church).

From 'an apostle of Jesus Christ' (v. 1)

This phrase tells us at least three things. First, Peter writes to us as a witness. That's what he tells us later in the letter (5:1), and that's what qualified him to be an apostle (see Acts 1:21–22). More than once as we go through this epistle we will have cause to remind ourselves of the experiences that lay behind some of his teaching.

Second, Peter was on a mission. The Greek word for

'apostle' (*apostolos*—our word 'apostle' comes straight from the Greek) means someone who has been set apart and sent out. In Peter's case, that sending can be traced back to Jesus' restoration of Peter recorded in John's Gospel. As he restored Peter, Jesus gave him his marching orders: 'Feed my sheep' (John 21:17); and in this letter Peter does just that. As sheep enjoying the love and care of the same Shepherd as the first recipients of this letter, we can expect to be fed as we study this part of Scripture.

Third, this phrase means that this letter comes with the authority of the one who sent Peter—Jesus Christ himself. So it demands our full attention, and calls for a response of firm faith and whole-hearted obedience.

From 'Babylon' (5:13)

Except that the letter doesn't come from Babylon. It's generally recognized that Peter is using 'Babylon' as a kind of symbolic code for Rome. Babylon had been the centre of the empire during Israel's years of exile, and Rome was the equivalent world capital in Peter's day. God's people faced a very different kind of 'exile' from the one Daniel experienced, but there are timeless principles which can be applied to any kind of suffering. Most believing commentators date Peter's letter during the reign of Nero, probably in the early 60s AD.

To ...

To the 'elect' (v. 1)

The term 'elect' has caused understandable difficulties for many over the centuries. After all, it is most commonly used in the context of elections, when people are voting for whoever they think is the most suitable candidate for a particular role. It would be a big mistake to think that the Bible's teaching on election has much to do with twenty-first-century forms of democracy. If the political arena isn't a helpful parallel, another example of electing or 'choosing' that might spring to mind is the picking of a football team in the school playground. Again, it's to do with identifying the best player available. It can be pretty disheartening if you're left until last; you're effectively being told that you're useless. It would be another big mistake for Christians to think that they have been chosen on account of their goodness, or even their potential. The Bible's idea of election contrasts with both examples because God chooses freely, without respect to the particular qualities possessed by any potential candidate. He chooses his people because he chooses them, and not for any other reason. As Paul puts it, '[God] has mercy on whomever he wills' (Rom. 9:14–18)—just decides 'for such [is his] gracious will' (Matt. 11:26). And that's just as well. If there were some clear criterion for being chosen, we can be sure that we would fall short of it.

> God chooses his people because he chooses them, and not for any other reason.

Those who try to explain away what the Bible teaches about election by claiming that God elects on the basis of what he foresees are mistaken. The story is told of a village in the Wild West. One day, a stranger came into town, and as he looked around he was immediately struck by the sight of numerous bullet holes in the wooden fences and gates. What was even more remarkable was that all the holes were located right at the centre of painted targets. The visitor, who considered himself a good shot, commented that he would love to meet the person who was responsible for such an impressive sight. You can imagine his surprise when he was then introduced to an eight-year-old boy. It turned out that the young lad shot the holes and then painted the targets around them! But election doesn't work like that; according to Scripture, it comes first. Christians aren't especially qualified, just especially loved.

Christians aren't especially qualified, just especially loved.

God knew the recipients of this letter from before the foundation of the world, knew all about them and their situation as Peter wrote, and also knew what they would face in the near future. But he not only knew them, he chose them.

To 'exiles' (v. 1)

'Elect exiles' sounds like a contradiction in terms, on a par with 'open secret' or 'small fortune'. How can somebody chosen by God end up facing life as an exile? We could tinker with the phrase to bring it closer to home. How about 'suffering Christian'? To much of the twenty-first-century church, that has a strange ring to it as well. If someone is a child of God, won't he or she be exempt from suffering? The combination may be initially puzzling, but it actually gets to the heart of Peter's first letter—and of the Christian life. Suffering is part of the Christian life—an important part.

The wonderful thing is that suffering has no part in the new heaven and new earth. In the meantime, while we are 'illegal aliens' (to use the American phrase) here on earth, we need a brutally honest travel guide to get us safely to our journey's end.

To 'the dispersion' (v. 1)

This was the common term used for Jews around the world after the Babylonian exile of the sixth century BC (see Jer. 25:34; Ezek. 22:15; John 7:35; James 1:1). But Peter sees the Christians of his day (the majority of whom were Gentiles) as a new *diaspora* (the Greek word behind our 'dispersion' which the Jews used specifically to describe their compatriots living in foreign lands, John 7:35; 11:52). Their true home isn't Jerusalem; it's heaven (Phil. 3:20). That's where they long to be and where they belong, where their heart is. The Welsh have a special word for it: *hiraeth*. Dr Martyn Lloyd-Jones, one of the most gifted preachers of the twentieth century, described his own experience of this at boarding school:

> *Hiraeth* is an awful thing, as also is the feeling of loneliness, and of being destitute and unhappy which stem from it. It is difficult to define *hiraeth*, but to me it means the consciousness of [a person] being out of his home area and that which is dear to him … My three years [at boarding school] were very unhappy and that was only because of this longing.[1]

So why does God allow this 'scattering'? Well, he more than allows it: he decrees it. The clue is in the word's origin. This scattering is a kind of sowing (*dia-spora*—to sow throughout). The book of Acts documents the way in which the gospel spread through scattering. As Christians were sent packing they sowed the seeds of the gospel:

- 'they were all scattered throughout the regions' (Acts 8:1);
- 'those who were scattered went about preaching' (Acts 8:4);
- 'those who were scattered ... travelled ... speaking the word' (Acts 11:19).

Thankfully, some of that seed falls on good soil and brings forth fruit—sometimes even a hundredfold (Matt. 13:23)! And often, persecution serves only to ensure a good harvest.

To those in 'Pontus, Galatia, Cappadocia, Asia, and Bithynia' (v. 1)

It must have seemed just a matter of time before these small groups of believers would be swallowed up by the hostile world around them. What chance did isolated members of a new sect stand against the might of the Roman Empire? Surely they couldn't last long. But Gamaliel was right: 'if ... this undertaking is of man, it will fail; but if it is of God, you will not be able to overthrow them' (Acts 5:38–39).

To those sanctified by the Spirit (v. 2)

They might have been scattered, but they were also special. They had been 'set apart', past tense. Often theologians use the term 'sanctification' (and associated words) to refer to the ongoing purifying work of the Holy Spirit in the Christian life. It's used in the Bible in that way at times, too, but quite often, as here, it is the initial work of 'setting apart' (the literal meaning of the Greek word translated 'sanctification') at conversion that is meant. This setting apart had been accomplished through the work of the Holy Spirit as the gospel was preached to them. It was similar to the way Peter had been set apart from his fishing on Galilee to instead become a fisher of men.

Peter then explains a twofold purpose behind this setting apart. First, it was for 'obedience' (even against a background of persecution). Second, it was for 'sprinkling'.

We will see that obedience is a theme of the whole letter, alongside suffering. As far as Peter is concerned, the greatest threat that difficulties pose is not the distress associated with them. His real concern is that such difficulties can divert us from the path of obedience. The plan of the Father and the work of the Spirit have put us on that path as followers of Christ. Peter wants us to stay on it, come what may. That's the aim. Thankfully, there is also provision for those times when our aim proves suspect. When the arrow falls short of the target, when we mess up, we can be sprinkled.

In the Old Testament, the sprinkling of blood was usually associated with the mercy seat. On only three occasions was blood sprinkled on the people themselves. The first is recorded in Exodus 24. It took place as part of the solemn confirming of the covenant between the Lord and the people. What made it so relevant to Peter's purpose here is that the sprinkling immediately followed Israel's pledge of obedience: 'All the words that the LORD has spoken we will do' (Exod. 24:3). The pledge was accompanied by offerings. Half of the blood from these offerings was thrown 'against the altar' (24:6); the other half was thrown 'on the people' (24:8). Immediately afterwards Moses said, 'Behold the blood of the covenant.' Peter is making the point to his readers that they are a covenant people too, equally committed to obedience. As they determine to follow the Saviour, Jesus says to them, 'This cup ... is the new covenant in my blood' (Luke 22:20).

The second time we read in Scripture of people being sprinkled is in connection with the consecration (or sanctifying/setting apart) of the priests. As Moses gave instructions to sprinkle blood 'on Aaron and his garments, and on his sons and his sons' garments with him' (Exod. 29:21), he explained the symbolic significance with the simple sentence, 'He and his garments shall be holy.' Again, Peter shows that this ancient ceremony has an application to his readers. Later in the letter he will explain that Christians have been made priests, and, having been set apart as holy, are now to live accordingly (1 Peter 2:5, 9–12).

The third situation in which someone was sprinkled with blood in the Old Testament was as part of the law for cleansing lepers. This was a sevenfold sprinkling which led to the leper being pronounced clean (Lev. 14:7). Just a few verses later we are told that the prescribed ceremony made atonement for the person concerned. The application for Peter's readers (and mine!) isn't hard to see. If you are a Christian, atoning blood has been applied, and the result is that you are clean.

With ...

With the prayer that 'grace and peace' will be 'multiplied' to them (v. 2)

True, Peter's readers had been chosen, set apart and sprinkled, but to hold to the path of obedience would not be easy. We need God's grace and peace multiplied to us because it's a hard and troubling road. But then, of course (as we'll see in the next chapter), it leads to a glorious destination that will make every inch of the perilous journey supremely worthwhile.

We will need God's grace to help us if we are to walk in God's ways. Life is an exam which comes in a multiple-choice format. If we are to keep making the right choices, the help which God gives will need to be multiplied as we come to one crossroads after another. And then there is the background of coming persecution which is never far from Peter's thoughts in this letter. To know God's peace in our hearts in the midst of many troubles requires a doubling or tripling of the Holy Spirit's peace-giving work within.

Peter knew what his readers would need, and prayed for it. Without it, they would become victims of persecution and hardship; with it, what lay ahead would serve only to strengthen their resolve and brighten their hope.

For further study ▶

FOR FURTHER STUDY

1. How many other examples can you think of or find in the Bible of people who had moments of great spiritual strength *and* of great weakness, like Peter?
2. Read Ephesians 4:20–32 and Colossians 3:5–17. What advice does the Bible give on how to put off the old man and put on the new man?
3. Read Romans 9:14–29. What objections to his teaching on election does Paul anticipate, and how does he answer them?
4. Where did the saying 'the blood of the martyrs is the seed of the church' originate? What are the most striking examples you can find of this in church history?

TO THINK ABOUT AND DISCUSS

1. In what ways does your 'old man' most often show himself?
2. In what areas of your life do you most struggle with obedience?
3. How does the 'sprinkling of blood' work out in our lives today? When does it happen? Do we need to do anything in order to be sprinkled? Should we expect to feel anything?
4. When you ask for God's grace (or help) to be multiplied, in what forms do you expect it to come?

Part 2
Salvation!

2 A praiseworthy salvation

(1:3–9)

Salvation! It's a word that is often over-used and under-appreciated. It gathers together in three syllables all that God has done, is doing and will do for us. Properly understanding each of those elements can put a song in our mouths and a spring in our step—even in the midst of trials.

A song of praise: our God (v. 3)

We often speak of the ways in which God blesses us. When we do so, we're usually talking about particular gifts that we have received from him. So at first, when we hear Peter telling us, his readers, to 'bless God', we might well wonder what he's talking about. How can we give anything to God? How can God be in need of anything from us?

Part of the confusion comes from the fact that there are two completely different Greek words that are both translated 'blessed' in most English Bibles. One relates to happiness and is used repeatedly in the opening section of the Sermon on the Mount. The Greek word is *makarioi* and speaks of a state of perfect satisfaction or happiness. We might, therefore, translate the Beatitudes in Matthew 5 with the words 'How happy are they who …' or 'Oh, the happiness of those who …' The Greeks gave the island of Cyprus the nickname 'the happy isle' (using this Greek word) because its climate and soil meant that it had everything it needed.

However, the word that Peter uses here is a different one. You have probably been to a funeral where somebody gave a 'eulogy'. That word comes from the Greek one employed by Peter here: *eulogetos*. It literally means 'to speak well of'. And, of course, that is what people generally do at funerals. The well-known proverb tells us not to speak ill of the dead; instead, we are supposed to speak well of them. Here, Peter wants God to be spoken well of—by us. It is an invitation to join Peter as he marvels at what God has done for us.

Peter doesn't want us to be in any doubt as to who this God is that he is extolling (literally, 'telling out about'). This is 'the God and Father of our Lord Jesus Christ'. The full title speaks of his divinity, humanity and anointed role as Prophet, Priest and King. Throughout the Old Testament, God had been known as 'the God of Abraham, Isaac and Jacob', revealed supremely in his covenant with them and their descendants. But those who have seen the Son have seen the Father (John 14:9) in a clearer way, and with a better covenant to boot. The Father's relationship with the Son, Peter seems to be saying, is what defines him more than anything else. And our relationship with the Son is what defines us.

Peter wants us to be equally clear about one of the reasons

we have to praise God. He has done something, and his mercy—'great mercy'—is the only explanation for it. He has 'caused us to be born again'. That in itself should be enough to get us singing, but the focus is on the result of that birth: hope—'a living hope'. The 'resurrection of Jesus Christ from the dead' is what really brings that hope to life. His resurrection guarantees our own, and assures us that death has been defeated. Paul tells us that, 'If in Christ we have hope in this life only, we are of all people most to be pitied' (1 Cor. 15:19). Thankfully, we don't: 'in fact Christ has been raised from the dead' (1 Cor. 15:20).

A song of heaven: our hope (v. 4)

The focus now switches from the one we hope in to what we hope for. Death is not the end. Beyond it lies an 'inheritance'—the substance of our hope. And it is truly substantial. The Greek word refers to an inherited property. Peter wants to show us around, and anyone with a living hope should never tire of taking a look.

Even though the inheritance is difficult to describe, the words just come tumbling out. Much as John struggles to describe the new heaven and the new earth in Revelation, so Peter can only talk of our hope by telling us what isn't true of it. It isn't perishable. Like God (Rom. 1:23; 1 Tim. 1:17), his word (1 Peter 1:23) and the crowns he awards (1 Cor. 9:25), it is not subject to decay. And we'll be supplied with a body to match, tailor-made for our new home (1 Cor. 15:52). 'Change and decay in all around I see,' said the hymnwriter,[1] but Peter (like Paul) is encouraging us to 'look not to the things that are seen but to the things that are unseen. For the things that are seen are transient, but the things that are unseen are eternal' (2 Cor. 4:18).

Not only will it never perish, but our inheritance isn't defiled. Israel, sadly, failed to heed the words of Moses (Num. 35:34; Deut. 21:23) and defiled the land (Jer. 2:7) that the Lord had given them for an inheritance (Deut. 4:20–21, 38; 12:9; 15:4; 19:10; 20:16; 21:23; 24:4; 25:19; 26:1). No such fate will befall the inheritance Peter is talking about. It will remain absolutely pure, with not the slightest hint of pollution from sin (just like our Saviour, Heb. 7:26). It will be pristine.

And it isn't going to fade. It will *remain* pristine. It won't be wonderful to start with, only for the magic to wear off with time. We're used to disappointment in this world. We gradually become accustomed to things and begin to take them for granted. We quickly lose interest in what seemed so exciting at first. Not so with our inheritance. John Newton wrote, 'Fading is the worldling's pleasure' and contrasted it with the 'solid joys and lasting treasure' that constitute the Christian's hope.[2] Great masterpieces fade and a huge amount has to be spent on their restoration in order to bring the colours back to life. Our hope is quite different. When we think about our inheritance, we often think of it as a vague, ethereal, shadowy existence, but Peter tells us that nothing could be further from the truth. This

When we think about our inheritance, we often think of it as a vague, ethereal, shadowy existence, but Peter tells us that nothing could be further from the truth.

world will be the one that is foggy and unreal by comparison. In *The Last Battle* C. S. Lewis has Aslan referring to what we call real life as 'the shadowlands'—a dream compared with the reality of glory.[3]

It isn't going to be full to capacity, either. As God's people we will each find that a reservation has been made in our name, with no double bookings. We may sometimes find the wait in this world something of a trial, just as heirs to a fortune may struggle with impatience, but the inheritance is in the safest of hands, being well managed until the day when it will become ours.

A song of safety: our confidence (v. 5)

'That's all very well,' we might say; 'I'm glad that the inheritance is safe, but what about me?' 'No need to worry about that,' Peter tells us; 'you'll be kept too.' How? 'By the power of God' comes the reassuring reply. Our level of confidence will fluctuate at times. There'll be times when we'll be perplexed. We may be quite clear about the promises of Scripture for the future, yet baffled by our circumstances in the present. We know that we have an inheritance reserved in heaven, but our cry is, 'What *on earth* is God doing right now?'

Peter gives us two answers to that question here. God is guarding us, and he is testing us. He is looking after us until the time when our ultimate salvation will arrive. It's ready, but it's not time yet. Only when it's time will it be fully 'revealed'. 'What we will be has not yet appeared …' (1 John 3:2). Until then, though, we are in safe hands. God will keep us.

The word 'guarded' here is a military one that speaks of

continual guarding (see 2 Cor. 11:32), and there is a particular means that God employs to do it. Our friendly bodyguard is 'faith'. Peter knew all about this. He needed to be kept, and the Lord told him how it would be done. The reason why Peter would emerge intact despite the devil's intentions and his own denials was because the Saviour 'prayed for' him, that 'faith [might] not fail' (Luke 22:32). Although looked at from one angle faith is 'the gift of God' (Eph. 2:8), it is a gift that we have a responsibility to exercise. 'Now faith', Hebrews tells us, 'is the assurance of things hoped for, the conviction of things not seen' (Heb. 11:1). So faith brings the inheritance closer; makes it real to us. It gives us a foretaste of that salvation which is tantalizingly ready and waiting, but will only be revealed 'in the last time'. We need to spend time thinking about the future—believingly.

A song of joy: our faith (vv. 6–9)

Hope mixed with faith is what turns a song of heaven into a song of joy. And it's a song which can be sung in the midst of 'various trials'. We don't rejoice in the trials themselves—we're not called to be masochists—but in the knowledge of what will come afterwards (the 'In this' of v. 6 refers back to vv. 4–5). As long as we grasp three things about our trials we should be able to carry on singing:

They will soon be over (v. 6)

Peter says they'll last only 'for a little while'. How does he know that for sure? Don't some trials go on for a painfully long time? Not in comparison with eternity. They may seem to be lasting an age as we go through them, but we will all agree in glory that they were 'momentary' and 'transient' (2 Cor. 4:17–18; see also Rom. 8:18). From an eternal perspective, our whole lifespan amounts to no more than 'a few handbreadths' (Ps. 39:5). It's easy to overlook the fact that in many parts of the world life is a struggle from cradle to grave. With faith and hope, though, things can begin to look very different.

You've probably heard of the Cape of Good Hope. What you might not be aware of is that its previous name was the Cape of Storms. It was renamed once it was known that beyond it lay the riches of the East Indies. Faith can turn our storms into times of 'good hope' too, as we look beyond them.

There is a necessity to them (v. 6)

Those two words in verse 6, 'if necessary', are easily missed but they tell us that God has a purpose in our trials. He uses them to accomplish things that nothing else can. There is a 'need be' concerning them (as the King James and New King James Versions put it). Sometimes they are broad providential purposes. The Lord's dealings with Joseph were 'to preserve … a remnant on earth, and to keep alive … many survivors' (Gen. 45:7) despite the famine. Sometimes it's more personal. Job said that his sufferings gave him a clearer view of God (Job 42:5), and the psalmist was able to say that his afflictions enabled him to learn and keep God's word (Ps. 119:67, 71).

> God uses trials to accomplish things that nothing else can.

To be forewarned is to be fore-armed. As the poet William Blake put it:

It is right it should be so;
Man was made for joy and woe;
And when this we rightly know,
Through the world we safely go.[4]

They are sent to test our faith (v. 7)

Just as gold is tested by fire, so faith is tested by trials, Peter says. He probably has in mind Job's words: 'when [God] has tried me, I shall come out as gold' (Job 23:10). Job emerged from his sufferings with his faith tried and tested. The devil had called the genuineness of his faith into question, but the trial he endured proved that it was the real thing. There is also a refining aspect to the testing of gold that can be applied to our afflictions as well, but Peter's focus is on genuineness. Emerging from tough times strengthens our own assurance (something Peter will have more to say about in his second letter; see 2 Peter 1:5–10), but also proves that our faith is the genuine article to a watching world (not to mention 'the rulers and authorities in the heavenly places', Eph. 3:10). And that will result in 'praise and glory and honour at the revelation of Jesus Christ'. It isn't clear whether this praise, glory and honour are for the believer or for the Lord. The context, Peter's word usage elsewhere and parallel Bible passages probably favour the former. Given that 'at the revelation of Jesus Christ' we will be free from pride and taken up with glorifying God, the distinction will be rather blurred then anyway. William Blake's faith passed the test. We are told that he died 'in a most glorious manner. He said

He was going to that Country He had all his life wished to see & expressed Himself Happy, hoping for Salvation through Jesus Christ—Just before he died His Countenance became fair. His eyes Brighten'd and he burst out Singing of the things he saw in Heaven.'[5]

What we should really be looking forward to is a clear sight of the Lord Jesus. At present we can't see him, but we do love him (v. 8). We can't see him, but we know what he has done for us. As with the inheritance, again it is faith that makes the difference. It not only gives us a joyous sense of anticipation of one day seeing our Saviour, but at times gives us a foretaste of that. There's a little bit of glory in the joy. It's all part of the process—a process of 'obtaining', little by little, a 'salvation' we will finally enter into in all its fullness when we *do* see him (v. 9).

On one occasion Bishop (and Professor) B. F. Westcott was passing an open-air Salvation Army meeting when one of the singers asked him whether he was saved. His reply was a characteristically theological one: 'Do you mean *esothain*, *sesosmai*, *sosomai*, or *sothesomai*?'[6] Thankfully, he went on to explain. The four Greek words are all different tenses of the word meaning 'salvation'. The first two cover the past ('Have you been saved?'), the third is the present ('Are you being saved?') and the fourth concerns the future ('Are you going to be saved?'). The Bible can talk about salvation in all three ways. From one angle it's in the past (Eph. 2:5, 8), from another it's an ongoing process (as here in Peter), and it can also be spoken of as future (Rom. 13:11). We should be thankful, and hopeful, even as we 'work out [our] own salvation' (Phil. 2:12)—joyfully.

For further study ▶

FOR FURTHER STUDY

1. What are the main themes in Psalm 103 where the psalmist is blessing God?
2. Find out as much as you can about the Greek word *eleos* that is translated as 'mercy'. What is a good definition, and what else does the New Testament tell us about God's mercy?
3. What do you think Paul was thinking about when he wrote 1 Corinthians 15:19? How would you use it to counter a 'prosperity gospel' that wrongly teaches that God always wants us to be healthy and wealthy? What other parts of Scripture would help to deal with this error?
4. Read Hebrews 12:5–14. What are we told here about God's purposes in trials? What encouragements and instructions are we given?
5. Read 2 Corinthians 12:1–9. What was the 'need be' to Paul's thorn in the flesh?
6. Who in the Bible can you think of who appeared to have genuine faith, only for it to be proved false when tested?

TO THINK ABOUT AND DISCUSS

1. Have you ever set aside time to think deliberately about the hope Scripture sets before us? What might help you to do so?
2. What disappointments have you faced? How does the Bible help us to deal with disappointment? In what ways does this world tend to disappoint us?
3. What is the difference between faith and wishful thinking?
4. What do you think is involved in working out our own salvation? Which Scriptures help us understand our responsibility in this, and which tell us about God's work, sometimes alongside us, and sometimes despite us?

3 A prophesied, purifying salvation

(1:10–21)

Peter has been surveying God's great plan of salvation, but he isn't the first to do so. The prophets had been doing it for centuries. Their vision was inspired but dim. Our view is clearer. And Peter tells us that the sight should be life-changing.

The prophets' message of grace (v. 10)

The salvation that Peter has been celebrating was no new-fangled idea. It had been a prophetic theme for centuries. The prophets themselves often had only a limited understanding of who they were speaking about, and were unclear about when their words would be fulfilled (Dan. 12:6, 8; Hab. 2:3; Matt. 13:17). Isaiah had sung his own song of salvation over 750 years earlier (Isa. 12:2–3). He was looking forward to a day ('that day', Isa. 12:1, 4) when God's anger would be turned away. That is a day that we, together with Peter and his readers, can look back on. Zechariah foresaw the arrival of salvation too—in the form of a king 'humble and mounted on a donkey' (Zech. 9:9). And the prophets spoke with one voice when it came to the source of this salvation: the grace of God. It wouldn't be deserved and couldn't be earned. It was, and is, a salvation 'without money and without price' (Isa. 55:1), and it would be based on a forgiving covenant (Jer. 31:31–34) in which the Lord multiplied gracious promises ('I will gather ... and I will give ... And I will give ... I will put ... I will remove ... and give ... and I will be their God', Ezek. 11:17–20).

The prophets' message of Christ (v. 11)

The message of the prophets wasn't just about a coming salvation, but about a coming Saviour as well. They talked about God's grace not just as a principle, but about God's Messiah—a person. Isaiah spoke of a 'Wonderful Counsellor, Mighty God, Everlasting Father, Prince of Peace' (Isa. 9:6) who would combine those roles with that of a servant (Isa. 42:1–4). Jeremiah spoke of 'a righteous Branch' that the Lord would raise up (Jer. 23:5), while Daniel saw 'one like a son of man' (Dan. 7:13), 'an anointed one, a prince' (9:25). Micah foresaw the emergence (from Bethlehem) of a 'ruler in Israel, whose coming forth is from of old' (Micah 5:2), and Zechariah relayed the Lord's words about 'my shepherd ... who stands next to me' (Zech. 13:7).

The prophets' message of sufferings and glories (vv. 11–21)

While they had a lot to say about who the Messiah would be, the prophets also had plenty to say about what he would do. Peter puts everything under two headings: 'sufferings' and 'glories' (v. 11). The glories were more prominent, but the sufferings were there for those with eyes to see, especially in Isaiah 53, but also in the (prophetic) twenty-second Psalm, and when we read of his being cut off (in Dan. 9:26) and struck (in Zech. 13:7). Some of the glories are described in Psalms 24 and 110, and Daniel got a clear sight of them too (7:13–14). But there was something important about the glories which Peter wants us to grasp: they were '*subsequent*' glories. The sufferings came first.

The sufferings come first for the Christian, too. That's what Peter wants to help us understand. He himself had found the prospect of Christ's sufferings hard to swallow (Matt. 16:22). The disciples the risen Lord met on the road to Emmaus also had to be taught the necessity of his suffering before entering 'into his glory' (Luke 24:26). They weren't ready for Christ's sufferings. Peter wants us to be ready for ours. One important part of coping with suffering is to keep in mind that, for the Christian, it will ultimately be followed by glory. The cross must come before the crown. It is a particular feature of 'this present time' (Rom. 8:18), but the future holds better things in store. There is even a sense in which the sufferings are so linked to the glory that follows that they can be described as 'preparing' it (2 Cor. 4:17). It is a package deal.

One important part of coping with suffering is to keep in mind that, for the Christian, it will ultimately be followed by glory.

What was revealed to the prophets of old was not

primarily for their benefit, but for the benefit of future generations (v. 12). Peter's readers were the true heirs of the Old Testament promises. They were also beneficiaries of the apostles' preaching and the ministry of the Holy Spirit. The clarity with which they could see was even greater than that enjoyed by angels (see Mark 13:32; Eph. 3:10; 1 Cor. 2:6–8). Such revelation was a privilege that came with a responsibility to think and act accordingly.

Be thoughtful (v. 13)

We have been 'born again to a living hope', but Peter now tells us that we have a responsibility to think about it. People who have a hope need to do some hoping. The kind of thinking needed will involve preparation, attention and focus. Spiritual thoughts seldom come easily to us; we need to be ready for some hard work. We might talk about 'pulling our socks up', 'rolling up our sleeves' or 'getting our thinking caps on'. In Peter's day they talked about 'girding up the loins of [their] mind' (ESV margin; literal translation of the Greek for 'preparing your minds for action') because of the way in which, in those days, they gathered up their clothes and tucked them into their belts. In the same way, Peter wants us to gather ourselves, and then gather our thoughts.

The word translated 'sober-minded' tells us that this needs to be serious thinking. We will need to be level-headed—not at the mercy of our feelings or moods, but prepared to think about God's promises, even when that's far from easy. Our thoughts need to be focused on what lies ahead. Grace is winging its way to us. It will arrive together with the revelation of the one we, as yet, have not seen (v. 8). Then we shall see him as he is (1 John 3:2). We should think about that a lot. We'll need determination and discipline ('set your hope'), and, to the exclusion of all distractions, we'll need to be focused ('fully').

Be holy (vv. 14–16)

But it's not just thinking that Peter is concerned about: there is also the important matter of obedience. It's a wonderful thing to know that you are a child of God, but then comes the question: What sort of a child are you? Peter wants us to be 'obedient children' (v. 14). A major part of growing up is learning to respect authority and to control yourself. We should be controlled by God's commands and not by 'the passions of [our] former ignorance'. 'Passions' stand in contrast to the 'hope' Peter is encouraging us to nurture. They are desires that demand instant gratification. But to cave in to their demands is to display an ignorance that should have been consigned to the past. In *Pilgrim's Progress* John Bunyan describes an important scene in a little room at the house of the Interpreter,

> where sat two little children, each one in his chair. The name of the eldest was Passion, and the name of the other Patience. Passion seemed to be much discontented, but Patience was very quiet. Then Christian asked, 'What is the reason of the discontent of Passion?' The Interpreter answered, 'The governor of them would have him stay for his best things till the beginning of the next year, but he will have all now; but Patience is willing to wait.'
>
> Then I saw that one came to Passion, and brought him a bag of treasure, and poured it down at his feet: the which he

took up, and rejoiced therein, and withal laughed Patience to scorn. But I beheld but a while, and he had lavished all away, and had nothing left him but rags.

The Interpreter then explains:

'These two lads are figures; Passion of the men of this world, and Patience of the men of that which is to come; for, as here thou seest, Passion will have all now, this year, that is to say, in this world; so are the men of this world: They must have all their good things now; they cannot stay till the next year, that is, until the next world, for their portion of good. That proverb, "A bird in the hand is worth two in the bush", is of more authority with them than are all the divine testimonies of the good of the world to come. But as thou sawest that he had quickly lavished all away, and had presently left him nothing but rags, so will it be with all such men at the end of this world.'

Then said Christian, 'Now I see that Patience has the best wisdom, and that upon many accounts. 1. Because he stays for the best things. 2. And also because he will have the glory of his, when the other has nothing but rags.'

'Nay, you may add another, to wit, the glory of the next world will never wear out; but these are suddenly gone.'[1]

An eternal perspective sees the importance of obedience.

In contrast to the short-termism of lust, an eternal perspective sees the importance of obedience. That is what true holiness consists of. It isn't some mystical experience or other-worldly demeanour; it is conducting ourselves in accordance with the Maker's instructions. To do that we will need to think straight, something that 'passions' are unlikely to help us with. We are supposed to bear the family likeness, which needs to be reflected in the nitty-gritty of everyday behaviour. Our thought-life is vital, but our conduct is equally crucial. It's a theme that Peter will return to later in his letter (vv. 17–18; 2:12; 3:1–2, 16). Our conduct must be holy (rather than 'futile', v. 18); honourable (2:12); pure (3:2); and good (3:16); the hope being that it will win over unbelievers (2:12; 3:1–2). The character of God calls for such obedience, and so do the Scriptures. 'It is written' (v. 16) stands as a bulwark against all our excuses for, and explaining away of, disobedience. It keeps us anchored while the values of society around us drift and standards of behaviour change. In the Scriptures we have objective and authoritative truth. And that will prove tremendously helpful in subduing our passions.

When the psalmist asks, 'How can a young man keep his way pure?' he supplies the answer, 'By guarding it according to your word' (Ps. 119:9). There's no getting around it: we are to be holy. We are to strive for holiness in every area of our lives ('in all your conduct'), and we should be in no doubt that it is essential (Heb. 12:14)—as are the Scriptures, if we are to make progress.

Be careful (vv. 17–21)

As well as thinking about our future hope, there is another aspect of the future that should occupy our minds and shape our lives: the prospect of judgement. That God is holy should affect our conduct; that he will be our judge should have an impact too. Thoughts of this coming judgement should make us careful—very careful—about the way we live our lives. There won't be any favouritism or special pleading on that day; deeds will be the basis of the ruling (v. 17).

If that isn't enough to motivate us, Peter reinforces his call to holiness with two further considerations. The first is the price that has been paid for our redemption; the second, the purpose for which it was paid. Peter began this section by using a phrase that harked back to the days of the exodus: 'girding up the loins' (v. 13, marginal reading, and see Exod. 12:11). Here Peter again draws parallels, with references to 'gold' and 'a lamb without blemish or spot' (vv. 18–19). If the deliverance at the exodus was great, the one that Peter's readers had experienced was greater. The blood of Christ is infinitely more valuable than the silver and gold 'ransom' of the exodus (Ps. 105:37; Exod. 12:35–36), and it was the purity of Jesus' life that made his sacrifice effectual in a way that the Passover lamb could only foreshadow.

Such a sacrifice! Offered to what end? To ransom us from our 'futile ways'. In other words, the ultimate purpose of Christ's sufferings was not simply to secure forgiveness, but to ensure that our lives would change. The 'futile [or vain] ways inherited from your forefathers' is almost certainly a reference to the idolatry of Egypt and, before that, Ur of the Chaldees.[2] That was all part of their 'former ignorance' (v. 14). A price had been paid so that things would now be different.

The sending of this wonderful Saviour was planned 'before the foundation of the world' (v. 20), but his mission had only just been accomplished, and it was all for them—for Peter's readers. The mission was, in a sense, incomplete without them. They were now 'believers in God' (v. 21). And with good reason. The resurrection and ascension demonstrated God's power and God's pleasure in the sacrifice of his Son. 'Faith' and 'hope' in such a God were well placed. Despite the sufferings that were still to be faced, they could be confident that they would not finally be put to shame or embarrassed. A living faith should make us hopeful about the future *and* obedient in the present.

For further study ▶

FOR FURTHER STUDY

1. How many different deliverances (national and personal) in the Old Testament can you identify that are referred to as examples of salvation? (Looking up 'salvation' and related words in a concordance should help.)
2. Read Colossians 1:24 and 2 Corinthians 4:16–17. In what way do our sufferings complete Christ's, and in what way are they preparing glory for us? What do we need to be especially careful to avoid as we interpret these two passages?
3. Read 1 Corinthians 10:1–12 and Romans 4:16–25. What are the main lessons for us from the Old Testament passages quoted? Do you think you would have understood their application to us without Paul's help?
4. Read Exodus 12:1–20. How many allusions to this passage can you find in the New Testament (a Bible with cross-references might help)? What are the main lessons for us?
5. Read Hebrews 12:14. How can holiness be essential without contributing to our salvation?
6. Read 1 Corinthians 3:10–15 and 2 Corinthians 5:9–10. What does the New Testament tell us about the judgement of believers?

TO THINK ABOUT AND DISCUSS

1. What promises regarding the future can you find in 1 Peter? How do they help, and in what circumstances are they especially helpful?
2. What passions affect our ability to think straight? How? Can you remember the last time you made a wrong choice because a strong desire wanting immediate fulfilment took control of you?
3. What modern-day examples of 'futile ways' can you think of?

4 A word-based, love-producing salvation

(1:22–2:3)

Martin Luther is said to have explained the Reformation with the comment, 'The Word did it all!' Peter says much the same thing in this section. The word of God brings new life, it brings growth, and it produces changed lives characterized by love.

A common experience (1:22–23; 2:3)

The scattered Christians of Pontus, Galatia, Cappadocia, Asia and Bithynia shared a common experience that Peter describes as 'obedience to the truth' (1:22). It's the same obedience that Paul speaks of as coming 'from the heart to the standard of teaching to which you were committed' (Rom. 6:17). It's the 'obedience of faith' (Rom. 16:26). The Bible sometimes describes the gospel as an invitation (Matt. 22:1–10), but it is also a command. It is a mistake to present the gospel in a 'take it or leave it' style, as if it is an optional extra. The urgency of the message calls for a response. 'Repent and believe!' is a command that is either complied with or rejected. Happily, Peter's readers had started as God meant them to go on—in obedience.

Peter has another way of describing this common experience in the next verse: they had been 'born again' (v. 23). Obedience to the truth is the first sign of new spiritual life. It marks a person's entrance into the kingdom of God. Jesus made it clear to Nicodemus that without this rebirth from above[1] the kingdom can't be seen, let alone entered (John 3:3). Clearly, being 'born again' is understood to be a profound experience—a radical new start.

Today, the term 'born-again Christian' is used to describe a particular 'type' of Christian, but according to the Bible every *genuine* Christian has been born again. To talk about a 'born-again Christian' is tautology—making no more sense than talking about a 'free gift', 'forward planning' or an 'armed gunman'.

The famous eighteenth-century preacher George Whitefield was once asked why he preached so often on John 3:7. He answered simply by quoting the text: 'Because "ye *must* be born again".'

Peter also characterizes this common experience, a few verses later, as a tasting 'that the Lord is good' (2:3). Here he is gently questioning whether his readers have been genuinely converted. If so, he says, they will have had a personal experience of God's goodness, as David did (Ps. 34:8).

A common blessing (1:22)

Not only did Peter's readers have a common experience,

they also shared a common blessing. A new start also meant a clean slate. They had 'purified their souls' (1:22).[2] That was some claim! Life for the Levitical priests in the Old Testament revolved around remaining ceremonially clean or pure[3] (see Lev. 8:15; Num. 8:21; Ezra 6:20; Neh. 12:30). Aaron was told, 'You are to distinguish between the holy and the common, and between the unclean and the clean' (Lev. 10:10). But cleanness was also to be a concern for the people. They were to watch their diet (Lev. 11), personal hygiene (chs 12; 15), health (13:1–14:32) and homes (14:33–53), to avoid uncleanness.

This concern for an outward, ceremonial cleanness was supposed to highlight a deeper, inward problem. What we need—and so obviously lack—is a clean heart. David felt it acutely after his sad fall. His prayer, 'Purge me with hyssop, and I shall be clean' (Ps. 51:7), is an allusion to the Old Testament laws for cleansing. He could have been thinking of either the handling of leprosy in Leviticus (Lev. 14:4, 6, 49, 51–52) or the red heifer purification rite of Numbers 19 (19:6, 18), or perhaps both. The latter was for those rendered unclean because of contact with a dead body. Whichever it was, David understood that the big issue is whether or not we have a 'clean heart' (Ps. 51:10). Job, centuries before, had asked, 'Can a man be pure before his Maker?' (Job 4:17), going on to answer with a very clear 'No!' (Job 15:14–15; 25:4; see also Prov. 20:9). We are all moral lepers, dead in trespasses and sins (Eph. 2:1), who have reason to pronounce ourselves 'Unclean, unclean' (Lev. 13:45). What Peter is telling us is that if we have obeyed the truth, then what the sprinkling of blood with hyssop symbolized has happened to us. The blood we have been sprinkled with is 'the precious blood of Christ' (1:19), and once we have been sprinkled with that (see Heb. 9:18–22; 10:22; 11:28; 12:24), our great high priest, along with Peter, declares us clean—'purified'. From then on, we have a responsibility (and should also have the desire) to purify ourselves in our daily lives (see 1 John 3:3; 2 Cor. 7:1), but that doesn't change the fact that we have been definitively purified. Jesus speaks about this in John 13: 'The one who has bathed does not need to wash, except for his feet, but is completely clean. And you are clean' (John 13:10). There is a decisive washing and then a continual, smaller-scale washing. There is the once-in-a-lifetime washing at conversion, followed by a daily washing from the dirt that we accumulate in everyday life.

There is the once-in-a-lifetime washing at conversion, followed by a daily washing from the dirt that we accumulate in everyday life.

This common experience and common blessing mean that the Christians Peter is writing to are part of the same spiritual family. They are now brethren,[4] and brethren need to get on ...

A common goal (1:22–23; 2:2)

'Brotherly love' is a goal of salvation. Having been 'born again', believers now have a common Father. As members of the same spiritual family, their relationships should be characterized by love. With a purified soul the Christian is now capable of the kind of love that comes 'from a pure heart'. While love usually should involve feelings, the Bible consistently places a premium on *commitment* and *action*. Biblical love consistently seeks the good of the other, even at our own expense. It consists of putting others first and ourselves second.

A number of Scriptures give us tests to check that our love is genuine. Sadly, there are a number of ways to fake the real thing, so Peter gives us some characteristics of true love. It's a love that is 'earnest'. The word in Greek has two elements to it—constancy and fervency. It doesn't come and go, and it isn't casual or shallow. There is an intensity and depth about it. This love is to have another rare quality: it is 'sincere'. Unlike much of the love we encounter in the world (and, sadly, the church has more than its fair share too), this love is to be 'unfeigned' or 'without hypocrisy' (the literal meaning of the Greek word). It doesn't cost us much to *appear* loving, and there are a whole host of reasons for our wanting to appear loving and be considered so by others—such as a desire for approval or popularity; but no ulterior motive should play a part in the love that we are to feel *and* show to our Christian brothers and sisters.

We can lose sight of the priority of love in the Christian life, even though the Bible does all it can to keep bringing us back to it (e.g. 1 Cor. 13). Maturity is all about love. That is why it is central to what Peter describes as 'grow[ing] up into salvation' (2:2). It is also at the heart of Paul's picture of maturity that he paints in Ephesians 4. If somebody is growing as a Christian, that person will become more loving, not less.

But where will the love come from? The problem is that

none of us are good at loving anybody other than ourselves. We just haven't got it in us. That's why we need outside help. And we get it from the word.

A common tool (1:22–25)

Earlier the stress was on what these Christians had been born again *to*—'a living hope'. In 1:23 Peter looks at where this new birth came *from*: the word of God. There is *life* in the word. The word of God was the tool employed by the Holy Spirit to bring the gift of new life (Titus 3:5). But the word's life-giving qualities aren't confined to that past event. It isn't just a kick-start to the Christian life: it is life-sustaining, as well as life-giving. It is vital for growth as well as birth. 'Man shall not live by bread alone, but by every word that comes from the mouth of God' (Matt. 4:4; Deut. 8:3). The word of God is living, and that means it is also active (Heb. 4:12). Here is a source of sustenance that is pure and which benefits us at the deepest level. What else can pierce 'to the division of soul and of spirit, of joints and of marrow … discerning the thoughts and intentions of the heart' (Heb. 4:12)? Having had a taste of the word at conversion, the healthy young believer will crave more. To neglect the Bible is to ensure stunted growth in the Christian life.

Another important quality that the word possesses is that it *lasts*. It is the 'abiding word of God' (v. 23). We don't abide, but the word does. It is 'imperishable'—it lives for ever. 'Heaven and earth will pass away, but my words will not pass away' (Matt. 24:35). That was Isaiah's point in these words quoted by Peter (1:24–25) that were written hundreds of years earlier. The Lord was speaking words of comfort to

Jerusalem (Isa. 40:1–11). The Lord their God was coming—they had his say-so to rely on. And it *was* reliable. Flesh, on the other hand, certainly isn't. Israel alternated between fearing the (very) human leaders of the countries around them and putting their trust in them. These leaders wouldn't last long, but 'the word of [their] God [would] stand for ever' (Isa. 40:8; 1 Peter 1:25). That the Lord was coming was 'good news' in Isaiah's day (Isa. 40:9). Peter tells his readers that the same 'good news' has been preached to them (v. 25)—only with a change of tense: the Lord *has* come!

A common problem (2:1–3)

'Grow up!' is usually the plea of a frustrated parent when a child fails to act his or her age. Peter wants to say much the same thing to his Christian readers. But before he does so, some preparatory work needs to be done. True, our souls were purified when we first believed, but impurities can very quickly contaminate the new heart of a young believer. The pollutants mentioned here all militate against the sincere, earnest and pure brotherly love that Peter is championing. He has already given us some of the positive qualities of true Christian love. Now he tells us what needs to be absent if the right kind of love is to be present (2:1).

Pure love leaves no room for 'malice', 'envy' or 'slander'. This unholy trinity moves from attitude to action. Wishing ill on others ('malice' or 'wickedness'—see Acts 8:22; Rom. 1:29; 1 Cor. 5:8; 14:20; Eph. 4:31; Col. 3:8; Titus 3:3; James 1:21; 1 Peter 2:16) and resenting success ('envy'—Matt. 27:18; Mark 15:10; Rom. 1:29; Gal. 5:21; Phil. 1:15; 1 Tim. 6:4; Titus 3:3; James 4:5) are attitudes that will eventually express themselves in words—'slander', 'evil speakings' (lit. 'speakings against'—2 Cor. 12:20; James 4:11; 1 Peter 2:12; 3:16).

If love is to be sincere, that also rules out 'deceit' and 'hypocrisy'. 'Deceit' refers to purposely misleading someone (Matt. 26:4; Mark 7:22; 14:1; John 1:47; Acts 13:10; Rom. 1:29; 2 Cor. 12:16; 1 Thes. 2:3; 1 Peter 2:22; 3:10; Rev. 14:5), while 'hypocrisy' literally means to put on an act that disguises what you really are or how you're really feeling (Matt. 23:28; Mark 12:15; Luke 12:1; Gal. 2:13; 1 Tim. 4:2; and Matt. 6:2, 5, 16; 7:5; 15:7; 16:3; 22:18; 23:13–15, 23, 25, 27, 29; Luke 13:15).

Peter isn't just informing us, though; he's exhorting us. Identifying these 'nasties' is only half the battle; they need to be 'put away'! Even though the word of God is active, we need to be active too. Thankfully, together with the outward help of God's word we can anticipate the inner help of the Holy Spirit as we get to work. The enlightening of God's word and the empowering of God's Spirit is a potent combination that can give us just the help we need.

FOR FURTHER STUDY

1. Read John 1:9–13. What do you think John is thinking about when he speaks of being born 'of blood', 'of the will of the flesh' and 'of the will of man'? Why was it so important to rule them out?
2. Read 1 Corinthians 13:4–8. Which of the characteristics of Christian love listed here do you think is most commonly overlooked in popular ideas about what love is?
3. Read 1 Corinthians 3:1–4. What are the symptoms of immaturity that Paul highlights here? What other signs of immaturity does Paul point to elsewhere in the same letter?
4. Read Matthew 23:1–28. What hypocrisies were the Pharisees guilty of?

TO THINK ABOUT AND DISCUSS

1. What would you say about your personal experience of God's goodness?
2. What can help us in the ongoing process of purification in our Christian lives?
3. What examples of hypocrisy have you come across in the media? Can you think of other examples in the church and in your own life?

5 A people-forming, excellency-proclaiming salvation

(2:4–10)

When we come to Christ we become part of a building project, and our Saviour has plans for us! He is building a new kind of temple—a spiritual one—of which each believer is a stone. And, like the original temple, it's to be a place for worship and witness.

Jesus had said many years before, 'I will build my church', and now Peter tells us how. First of all, we have to come to Jesus (v. 4); then the work of construction really gets under way. The project, though, is a spiritual one, and the blueprints are found in the Old Testament. The priesthood at that time offered animal sacrifices to point forward to Christ; the priesthood Peter is talking about here offers *spiritual* sacrifices. The acceptability of those sacrifices depends upon the 'once for all' (Heb. 9:12, 26; 10:10) sacrifice of Calvary. In fact, everything depends upon Christ. He is the stone without which there is no building and no salvation.

Who we have come to

Jesus is 'a living stone' (vv. 4, 6–7, 9)

Jesus is the stone Isaiah talked about hundreds of years before; a stone that Israel had sung about over the centuries in one of their psalms. Those ancient prophecies told of two very different attitudes towards the same stone. Psalm 118 prophesied that it would be rejected by the builders (v. 22). Peter had heard Jesus quote that psalm to explain what was about to happen to him (in the parable of the tenants, Matt. 21:33–44). And Peter had quoted it to the rulers and elders just after Pentecost (Acts 4:11). They were the very ones who had done the rejecting, just as Jesus had foretold: 'the Son of Man must suffer many things and be rejected by the elders and the chief priests and the scribes and be killed, and after three days rise again' (Mark 8:31; see also Luke 9:22; 17:25). The opposite of rejecting this living stone is to 'receive him' (John 1:12), or, as Isaiah and then Peter put it, 'believe in him' (Isa. 28:16; 1 Peter 2:6). Those who put their trust in the living stone will 'not be put to shame'; on the contrary, 'honour' is their lot (see 1 Peter 2:7). It is the honour of belonging to him and of bearing his name—being one of the 'chosen race, a royal priesthood, a holy nation' (v. 9).

Jesus is a 'stumbling' stone (v. 8)

When he is rejected there are consequences. If a positive response to the gospel can be described as 'obedience to the truth' (1:22), the flipside is that unbelief involves disobeying the word, and that can only spell disaster—a fall from which, unless repented of, there can be no recovery. The word says 'Receive!' (e.g. John 1:11–12), but the response is often one of rejection. The word says 'Come!', but many won't (see John 5:40). The word says 'Believe!', but people make their excuses. Many take offence at the person of Christ, unwilling to look beyond his humanity to his divinity (Mark 6:3). But it is his work on the cross that proves especially hard to swallow for some (1 Cor. 1:23). Paul calls it 'the offence of the cross' (Gal. 5:11). It was especially offensive to the Jews of the first century in certain ways, but it continues to be offensive in the twenty-first century. The need for faith in 'Christ crucified' (1 Cor. 1:23) is, for many, a bridge too far. Pursuing salvation by works comes naturally; nobody is offended by that. But faith *alone* is another matter. It involves eating a large slice of humble pie.

The need for faith in 'Christ crucified' is, for many, a bridge too far.

These negative responses come as no surprise to God. He doesn't delight in the death of the wicked (Ezek. 18:23, 32) but it is still true that their fate was pre-'destined' (1 Peter 2:8). His divine, sovereign plan is being worked out, without that in any way removing our individual responsibility. Those who stumble will ultimately be ashamed of themselves (Isa. 28:16)[1]—not because they weren't chosen, but because of the wrong choices they made. Those who do believe will come to realize that they owe everything to God's choosing grace. Yes, they, in time, chose the Saviour, but only because he, before time, chose them (John 15:16).

Jesus is a 'cornerstone' (vv. 5–10)

Jesus is not just any cornerstone, but one that is 'chosen and precious' (v. 6). He was 'despised and rejected by men' (Isa. 53:3), but in the sight of God he was 'chosen and precious'. He was chosen—like David (1 Sam. 16:8–13; see also Isa. 43:10; Matt. 12:18; Luke 9:35; 23:35); chosen—as Isaiah had prophesied of the Lord's servant (Isa. 42:1); and precious—like Isaiah's stone (Isa. 28:16). So how did this rejected stone 'become' the cornerstone (2:7; Ps. 118:22; Acts 4:11)? Peter's answer is, 'Through the resurrection!' That's when his acceptance by God was made clear. That's when he was 'declared to be the Son of God in power' (Rom. 1:4). It was a divine reversal of man's rejection. The choir of a church in Hampshire once performed Stainer's *Crucifixion*, after which the conductor put up a notice saying '*The Crucifixion*—Well done everybody!' By the end of the day, someone had written underneath, 'The Resurrection—Well done God!' Whoever it was, the culprit had a point.

There is some debate about the function of the cornerstone in the building projects of Isaiah's day, but the basic point is clear. Whether it was in a foundational role or as the stone from which the position of all other stones was calculated, the stone was vitally important.

There is an old Jewish legend that, when Solomon's temple was being built, the workmen from the quarry sent a stone to the temple site. It was an unusual shape, and no one there knew what it was for, so the stone was put to one side. When the temple was nearly finished a request arrived at the quarry for the capstone of the key arch. The reply eventually came back that the capstone had already been sent. The workmen at the temple were puzzled. They didn't have it, and they couldn't see it. But then one of them remembered the odd-shaped stone that had been quickly discarded. A team was despatched to retrieve the stone that had been thrown away, and sure enough it was the keystone they had been looking for (see Ps. 118:22).

Who we have become (2:9)

We are a chosen race

The fact that Peter's readers believed in the 'cornerstone' told them that they were 'chosen and precious' just like Jesus. The Lord had reassured Israel hundreds of years earlier, through the prophet Isaiah, of the same thing (Isa. 43:4, 20; see also Deut. 10:15). Describing his readers as 'a chosen race' (v. 9) is daring language when addressing Gentiles and Jews together, all the more so as 'family' is probably a better translation (see Acts 4:6; 7:13).

We are a royal priesthood

Peter proceeds to rattle off a number of other titles used of the people of God in the Old Testament, applying them to his readers, the 'living stones' in this new spiritual building. They had the privilege of being part of 'a royal priesthood' (see Exod. 19:6) that the original temple priesthood could only foreshadow. Peter had already referred to them as a 'holy priesthood' (v. 5). The word 'holy' speaks of being set apart (or 'consecrated', as it is translated in the Old Testament with reference to the Levitical priesthood, Exod. 28:3) for the service of God. That service revolved around *offerings*, and Peter has already explained how that applies to Christians by mentioning the 'spiritual sacrifices' they have to offer (v. 5). Hebrews tells us that these include giving 'praise to God', doing good and sharing (Heb. 13:15–16). The other aspect of priesthood which clearly prefigures our Christian privileges is that of *access*. Only the priests could enter the holy place in the tabernacle. It was quite an honour—and yet they couldn't just stroll in whenever they wanted to; there was a complex procedure that needed to be followed. For us, though, the way has been opened up by our great high priest (Heb. 10:20). As a result, instead of feeling the fear and trepidation with which the priests of the Old Testament entered the sanctuary, 'we have confidence to enter the holy places by the blood of Jesus' (Heb. 10:19). We have 'obtained access by faith' (Rom. 5:2), and it's unlimited access, 24/7.

But Christians now constitute not just a holy priesthood, but a *royal* priesthood. The whole nation of Israel (not just the priests) had been described as 'a kingdom of priests' (Exod. 19:6). We've also entered a kingdom, and one of the amazing differences between the two kingdoms makes the Septuagint[2] rendering of Exodus 19:6 that Peter quotes especially appropriate. We are not just a kingdom made up of priests, but we are a *royal* priesthood, because every single subject of this kingdom is a child of the King.

We are a holy nation

We belong to the 'holy nation' that is now being formed. We are now 'a people for his own possession', as Israel had been centuries before (Deut. 7:6; see also Exod. 19:5). Our job is the same: to 'proclaim the excellencies' of God (see Isa. 43:21).

The challenge is to try to do a better job than Israel did. As witnesses, God's people had failed miserably throughout the Old Testament. They were supposed to keep God's commandments before a watching world (Deut. 4:6). Instead, their disobedience meant that the Lord's name was in danger of being 'profaned in the sight of the nations' (Ezek. 20:14, 22). That was why the Lord sent his servant—to be the 'light for the nations' that Israel had failed to be (Isa. 42:6). Isaiah goes on to tell us how the Lord's special servant would call people out of darkness: 'saying to the prisoners, "Come out", to those who are in darkness, "Appear"' (49:9). Isaiah also tells us about 'the glory of the LORD' which would one day rise on the covenant people (60:1). 'The LORD will be your everlasting light' (60:19–20) were Isaiah's words—what Peter calls 'his marvellous light' (v. 9). The transformation Isaiah prophesied is what Peter's readers have experienced. And Isaiah wasn't the only one who saw it coming: Hosea foresaw it too (Hosea 1:10; 2:1)— this time, not in terms of darkness and light, but of Jew and Gentile. Peter is telling us that the times Isaiah and Hosea glimpsed have now arrived. But receiving mercy (v. 10) is only the beginning. Peter is going to help us understand how to set about proclaiming God's excellencies—how to be the witnesses we're called to be.

The Greek word translated 'proclaim' (v. 9) is an unusual one and had the sense of 'publishing' or 'advertising' something that was otherwise unknown. The idea of a press release today perhaps gets close to the meaning of the original. In short, God's people have an announcement to make. We should be keen to *tell* people about 'the excellencies' of our God. There is a beauty and a glory about the God of the Bible

Every Christian, then, should be a walking, talking advert for the good news about the goodness of God.

that we want others to see. So we talk the talk, but we also need to walk the walk. Our lives should be a kind of statement. People should be able to learn something by seeing how Christians live their lives. We should *reflect* his excellencies. Some we can't reflect (those that are often referred to as God's 'incommunicable attributes'[3]), but some we can (his 'communicable attributes'[4]). Every Christian, then, should be a walking, talking advert for the good news about the goodness of God.

You're writing a Gospel,
A chapter each day,
By the deeds that you do,
By the words that you say.

Men read what you write,
Whether faithless or true;
Say, what is the 'gospel'
According to you?[5]

Proclaiming the excellencies of God isn't just about focusing on God's abstract qualities. We're supposed to be witnesses, and that means speaking of what this amazing God has done *for us*. He has changed our lives; he can change the lives of others, too. He has called us 'out of darkness into his marvellous light'. We used to be our own bosses, but now we belong to him. Best of all, our greatest need has been met: we have 'received mercy' (v. 10).

For further study ▶

FOR FURTHER STUDY

1. Read Philippians 4:16–17; Romans 12:1; Hebrews 13:15–16. What spiritual sacrifices are we supposed to offer? What else might count?
2. Read Romans 9:32 and 11:11. What, specifically, about the gospel caused many Jews to stumble? What was God's overarching purpose in this stumbling?
3. Draw up a list of God's communicable and incommunicable attributes (consulting a systematic theology or the Internet may help!).

TO THINK ABOUT AND DISCUSS

1. What, generally, do people find most offensive about the gospel today? In what ways can we sometimes be unnecessarily offensive in the way we present the good news?
2. What do you immediately think of when somebody mentions 'holiness'? How does it differ from the Bible's teaching about what constitutes holiness?
3. How good do you think the church today is at proclaiming God's excellencies to unbelievers? How might it improve?
4. Which of God's excellencies do you think you are in a particularly good position to explain to others, because of your own experience?

Part 3
Conduct!

6 Honourable conduct

(2:11–17)

Not only have Christians become part of a building project, but also they are now 'sojourners and exiles', and that has all sorts of implications. It places them in the midst of a raging battle and puts them on exhibition before a watching world. How they conduct themselves in the light of all this will prove crucial.

Travellers (v. 11)

God's people have been pilgrims ever since Abraham confessed himself to be 'a sojourner and foreigner' (Gen. 23:4). The time Israel spent in Egypt is referred to as a 'sojourn' (Gen. 47:4; Deut. 10:19), but even as Moses gave instructions for life *in the land* he told Israel, 'you are strangers and sojourners with me' (Lev. 25:23). The message was clear: even Canaan wasn't their ultimate destination. Abraham had recognized this long before. How clearly he understood is open to debate, but the letter to the Hebrews leaves us in no doubt that Abraham saw beyond the physical fulfilment of God's promise to a spiritual one (Heb. 11:8–10, 13–16).

Our sight, with all the help of the New Testament, is certainly much clearer. The word 'sojourner' (v. 11) stresses the temporary nature of someone's stay; the word 'exiles'[1] focuses on the alien environment in which that person dwells. The words of the gospel song capture both aspects (though in reverse order): 'This world is not my home; I'm just a-passing through.'[2] Peter wants us to grasp that our status as sojourners and exiles should have a profound effect upon our conduct. Our attitude and approach to life should be quite different from that of people who believe that 'this is all there is'.

I am writing these words in a hotel room. I plan to be here for two nights only, so I am not too fussed about the facilities or the decor. If I was staying for a year or moving in permanently, I would be a much more difficult customer. The length of my stay has a real impact on my behaviour. I'm not settling down: I'll be gone in a couple of days; there's no need to complain about minor inconveniences.

Even if we live to be a hundred our lives are exceedingly brief in comparison with eternity. Our stay in this world is fleeting, and we aren't supposed to feel at home here. In fact, the Bible warns us that it is a very bad sign if we do.

Abstainers (v. 11)

Those with the right perspective value their souls. After all, the soul is eternal. It's well worth looking after your body if you want it to function relatively well for most of your life, but your soul is eternal—it deserves infinitely more care and attention. Nowadays, things that are bad for the body often carry health warnings, but here Peter is issuing a health warning for the soul. Sojourners and exiles will want to avoid anything that could harm their souls. Peter warns us about 'the passions of the flesh'. They don't just damage, they 'war against' the soul. Here Peter uses a word that was employed in the context of a long-term military campaign. We will need to be on our guard for the long haul.

They look very attractive, and they don't advertise the hurt they can cause, but 'passions' aggressively attack our spiritual well-being. There is, perhaps, little need to go into detail about what 'the passions of the flesh' are; we are probably all too familiar with them. But it is worth noticing that for Paul they extended beyond the class of sins that we might immediately think of. In his letter to the Galatians he makes it clear that 'enmity, strife, jealousy … rivalries, dissensions' are included (Gal. 5:20). Peter's advice is as heartfelt (indicated by the Greek word translated 'urge', v. 11) as it is straightforward: 'Abstain!' Self-control will be required—the word translated 'abstain' literally means 'hold oneself off', or we might translate it 'refrain from'. This kind of sin has both a pulling power and a corrupting, spreading influence. 'Abstain, or be stained!'

Witnesses (v. 12)

Caring for our souls is one motive, but Peter also supplies another. The effect that sin can have on us is certainly one consideration, but the way in which it affects our witness is another. 'Honourable' conduct is what is called for, but especially because life is lived 'among the Gentiles' (or, for most of us in our situations today, 'among unbelievers'). That is how it should be[3]—but, sadly, we are not always what we should be. Dishonourable conduct has the unhappy effect of causing the enemies of God to blaspheme—that is, to speak badly of the God who is being so poorly represented. In short, dishonourable conduct dishonours God (see especially Rom. 2:24; 1 Tim. 6:1; Titus 2:5).

Honourable conduct, on the other hand, won't stop unbelievers speaking badly about the people of God, but it will trouble their consciences, and quite possibly lead them to respond positively to the gospel at some point in the future. Church history abounds with examples of people who, like Saul of Tarsus, at one time persecuted Christians, but then after a period of 'kicking against the goads' had a 'road to Damascus' kind of 'day of visitation' (v. 12).

Citizens (vv. 13–15)

If passions of the flesh are, negatively speaking, a danger area that can lead to *dis*honourable conduct, clearly Peter sees our responsibilities as citizens to be a crucial positive component of honourable conduct. Through the ages Christians have endured many false accusations about their attitude to the state. They have often been portrayed as unpatriotic, rebellious, revolutionary and dangerous. Peter is concerned that the Christians he is writing to do not give any ammunition to their enemies in this area. Christians are to be fine, upstanding citizens. And if they are worried that they might be compromising, Peter has some reassurance for them: their subjection to the emperor, or lesser governors, is 'for the

Lord's sake' (v. 13). That is to be their motivation. There is a very real sense in which these civil authorities are 'sent by him' (v. 14). And they are sent with a particular job to do: 'to punish those who do evil and to praise those who do good'. How well they fulfil their God-given role is not the point. After all, Peter was probably advocating the honouring of the emperor during the reign of Nero (though probably before the persecution of Christians began in earnest). Pontius Pilate had authority that he had received from God, and he would be judged according to his use or abuse of that authority (John 19:11). The high priest Caiaphas would be tried on the same basis, but Jesus tells us that his sin was the greater (John 19:11). Abuses, though, do not excuse us from our responsibility to submit to the authorities. They are in charge, and they are supposed to be in charge. We are supposed to be subject to them.

The only scenario in which Scripture tells us we are to act contrary to governments is when their authority clashes directly with that of God himself.

The only scenario in which Scripture tells us we are to act contrary to governments is when their authority clashes directly with that of God himself. The same Peter who wrote this letter could say to the Jewish council in Jerusalem, 'Whether it is right in the sight of God to listen to you rather than to God, you must judge' (Acts 4:19). Otherwise, 'doing good' as an obedient and respectful citizen 'is the will of God' (1 Peter 2:15). Our subjection is 'for the Lord's sake'. It is our subjection to him that determines our subjection to the authorities. 'Doing good' has a particular aim in view: to 'put to silence the ignorance of foolish people' (v. 15). It will (literally in the Greek) 'muzzle' their detractors. Rather than fuelling the accusations of their enemies by rebellious or revolutionary activity, Peter's readers are to quench them with irreproachable behaviour.

We are to be like Daniel. His enemies 'sought to find a ground for complaint' against him (Dan. 6:4). Many a politician or celebrity has been unable to survive similar scrutiny from the press, but Daniel was different. What a wonderful testimony to have: 'they could find no ground for complaint or any fault, because he was faithful'! His one area of weakness, from their point of view, was, in fact, his strength: 'We shall not find any ground for complaint against this Daniel unless we find it in connection with the law of his God' (Dan. 6:5). May the same be said of us!

Free bondservants (vv. 16–17)

Being subject to human institutions is rarely popular teaching. 'But that makes us no better than servants of the state!' someone cries. 'Far from it!' is Peter's reply. You are really 'servants of God' (v. 16). The paradox is that to be a servant of God is to know true freedom. The psalmist, long before, had observed, 'I will walk at liberty, for I seek Your precepts' (Ps. 119:45, NKJV). Without God's help we are slaves to sin, even though we might think that we are doing just as we please. That, according to Scripture, is the very worst kind of bondage.

Freedom is a concept that we can easily get wrong. It can be used to justify all sorts of questionable practices. If we are not careful, Peter warns us, we can end up using 'freedom as a cover-up for evil'. Church history and twenty-first-century church life has produced a number of high-profile casualties who have had a lot to say about the Christian's freedom, only to be ultimately exposed as secret evildoers. Freedom is all about what you do with it. We have to be careful when talking about our having free will. If by using that term we mean that the choices we make in life are made by us willingly, unforced by outside influence, then that is true. But this doesn't mean that we are outside of God's sovereign control; nor does it mean that we are free from our own drives and desires when making choices. That is why theologians have talked about 'the bondage of the will'. We are free to choose, but our desires will generally dictate the choices we make. We are free, but we are unable to use that freedom to choose what is right without outside help. Those who are servants of God, however, have all the help they need at their disposal. The freedom we enjoy is a freedom from man-made rules (Gal. 5:1, 13), but not a freedom to commit sin—or to disrespect others. Honourable conduct involves honouring people (1 Peter 2:17). Peter almost certainly has in mind here the teaching of our Saviour, when he taught about 'render[ing] to Caesar the things that are Caesar's' (Matt. 22:21). This honouring, however, needs to be matched with a love for our fellow Christians and a deep reverence for God.

FOR FURTHER STUDY

1. Read Romans 2:23–24. What kinds of law-breaking did Paul have in mind here?
2. Read 1 Timothy 6:1. What would be the application of this teaching today?
3. What biblical examples can you find of people from the surrounding nations being critical of the morality of God's people?
4. Read Matthew 22:15–21. What is the significance of the likeness and inscription on the coin?

TO THINK ABOUT AND DISCUSS

1. What difference does it make to the way you live your life to know that you are just 'passing through' this world?
2. What things around you have the potential to damage your soul? What precautions can you take?
3. What examples of being a bad witness to unbelievers have you come across?
4. What limits are there for the Christian when it comes to being 'subject' to civil authorities?
5. What does 'render[ing] to Caesar the things that are Caesar's' involve today?

7 Enduring conduct

(2:18–25)

Honourable conduct as a citizen of the Roman Empire was one thing, but a Christian worker's relationship with his master was another challenging area, one equally important in terms of witness to a watching world.

Suffering for the right reason (vv. 18–20)

The Christian must expect suffering, but Peter is concerned to ensure that none of it is self-inflicted. He doesn't want us to be bad citizens; if we are, then we only have ourselves to blame when punished by the authorities. More importantly, it is a bad witness. Now Peter wants us to be careful to be good workers, model employees. If you're a lazy, scowling servant, then you can complain about religious persecution all you like when you face discipline from your master, but the problem lies with you. In our day, this discipline may be in terms of a fine, a demotion or a formal caution; in Peter's day it meant a beating (v. 20). Either way, there is nothing praiseworthy about enduring a punishment you have well and truly earned. Our responsibility as Christians is to make sure that we are doing good, whatever our enemies might say and do. If we can tick that box, then 'enduring' is the name of the game (v. 20). We will need to keep going, to exhibit stamina or staying power. The Greek word used for 'endure' here means literally to 'stay under' and implies a pressurized situation in which we persevere (see Rom. 12:12; Heb. 10:32). Sometimes translated 'patient endurance', it's the word James uses to sum up the fortitude of Job (translated 'steadfast' and 'steadfastness' in the ESV, James 5:11). Hebrews applies the same word to our supreme example. Jesus 'endured the cross' (Heb. 12:2), and considering him (12:3) will help us run *our* race with the endurance we'll need (12:1).

The 'doing good' as a servant that is needed consists of respectful subjection to your master (1 Peter 2:18). That isn't easy, and our instinctive reaction may be a string of 'but's. The classic get-out is, 'Ah! But you don't know what my master is like! You can't seriously be telling me that I've got to submit to such an unreasonable bully!' Peter wisely blocks off that way of escape: 'not only to the good and gentle but also to the unjust'. Subjection—a commitment to obedience—is not optional. The Greek word translated 'subject' has the literal meaning of being 'set under' and was used in a military context for the arrangement of soldiers in formation under a commander. Whichever way you look at it, the word establishes an authority structure.

We are rarely comfortable being 'under' anybody else. Couple that with a society that is, at best, suspicious of authority in general, and we can anticipate objections—especially as this term is applied in so many different areas. The general need of mutual submission is taught in Scripture, but there is a specific responsibility within certain relationships that is sometimes explained away by appealing to the more general references. The truth is that none of us are exempt from this duty. Whoever we are, whether citizens, servants, wives or just plain Christians (Eph. 5:21), we will need to learn the art of submitting. The Latin origin of our word 'submit' (literally 'send under' or 'place ourselves under') closely parallels the Greek word. A road sign that we see everywhere can serve as a reminder of the whole concept: 'Give Way!' (or 'Yield' in the USA). That doesn't come easily to most of us. Being a rare quality today it poses some challenges, but it does provide us with an opportunity to stand out; to 'shine as lights' 'in the midst of a crooked and twisted generation' (Phil. 2:15).

Suffering with the right attitude (vv. 18–19, 21)

Being obedient to the state is important, but mere outward compliance isn't enough. It needs to be combined with the right inward attitude. This is where Christianity is so demanding. The heart, not just the actions, has to be right. 'Respect' is essential (v. 18). A servant who gets the work done, muttering under his breath as he does it, and who makes fun of his master as soon as his back is turned, is falling far short of the biblical standard.

The master's shortcomings are not the issue. It is our responsibility to be good servants; it is the master's responsibility whether or not he is a good master. There may be no immediate reward (maybe quite the opposite) for enduring harsh and unfair treatment from an employer, but it pleases God. He notices. That carries weight with those who are 'mindful of God' (v. 19)—otherwise, it makes little sense. The world will think you are a fool; your master may do too, but he will acknowledge (though, perhaps, only to himself, and that grudgingly) that your attitude as a servant cannot be faulted.

A twenty-first-century employer–employee relationship differs from the first-century master–servant one in a number of respects, but the principle here holds good. The Christian should be a good worker, even when he or she has a bad boss. At times in history, people who have been no friends of Christianity have been forced to confess that Christians make the most honest, reliable and diligent workers. As we saw in the last chapter, Daniel got a reference from his enemies, and his king, that should be that of every Christian: 'We shall not find any ground for complaint against this Daniel unless we find it in connection with the law of his God' (Dan. 6:5).

The Christian should be a good worker, even when he or she has a bad boss.

We instinctively feel that something is wrong when we face injustice in the workplace, but Peter assures us that it is exactly what we should expect. The Christian's calling is to endure just such situations (v. 21). How we handle them is a good test of our claim to be Christ's disciples. Are we the real thing? If we fail at this point, then we are, at best, lacking maturity. What we don't lack is the perfect example ...

Suffering with the right example (vv. 21–24)

Our Saviour knows all about suffering—especially that of the unjust variety. Of course, bearing the punishment our sins deserve was the most important aspect of his sufferings from our point of view. Nonetheless, they also have a role to play in serving as an example to us. That is what Christ intended, Peter tells us. As he thinks about suffering, his mind turns to a classic passage in the Old Testament on the subject, one that has been brought into clear focus by the crucifixion: Isaiah 53. Never was there a better example for Peter's purposes. Jesus managed to remain sinless in the most unjust of situations, under the most extreme provocation. He didn't *do* anything wrong, but Peter stresses that he didn't *say* anything wrong either (vv. 22–23): no deceit, no reviling, no threatening. Peter is quoting Isaiah 53:9, but he was probably thinking about 53:7 as well: 'there was no deceit in his mouth ... like a sheep that before its shearers is silent, so he opened not his mouth ...' Peter sees that Isaiah 53 described the perfect sufferer—'a man of sorrows' (53:3). One of the most impressive things about the Lord at the time of his suffering was his silence. When you can't do anything about injustice, you instinctively want to give vent to your feelings, to have your say. At the cross, the thieves on either side of the Saviour resorted to reviling (Mark 15:32). Jesus was different; he didn't respond in kind.

To suffer in silence is not easy. How did Jesus do it? It was a matter of trust. That's how we'll manage to hold our peace, too. We need to trust 'him who judges justly' (v. 23). We need to commit our cause—and our spirit—into God's hands.

Another scene from the cross, prophesied hundreds of years before, springs to Peter's mind. Psalm 31:5 was quoted by the Lord as his sufferings came to an end. It is the language of trust. In fact, the very next verse of the psalm contains the affirmation, 'I trust in the LORD' (Ps. 31:6; see also v. 14). First Jesus had been delivered 'into the hands of men' (Matt. 17:22; 26:45, 50; Mark 9:31; 14:41; Luke 9:44; 24:7), but as his sufferings drew to a close he entrusted his spirit into the hands of his Father (Luke 23:46). There is no safer pair of hands. And this wasn't a one-off committing or commitment: Peter uses the imperfect tense—he 'continued entrusting'—and so must we.

Trusting generally involves waiting (as the close of Psalm 31 reminds us—v. 24). God will sort it all out, but not necessarily as soon as we would like. Still, there *will* be a day of reckoning—and that means we don't have to insist on justice here and now, or even fret when we are unfairly treated. God knows; and one day he will put things right.

The cross sets us free from condemnation, but it also sets us an example. Next, Peter points out that it has another purpose: Jesus died for our sins so that 'we might die to sin' (v. 24): to set us increasingly free from sinning, and to set us increasingly right. Peter still has the words of Isaiah in mind as he says, 'He himself bore our sins' (compare Isa. 53:4, 6, 12), along with a reference to Moses when he tells us that it took place 'on the tree' (Deut. 21:22). But it was all with an end in view: 'that we might die to sin and live to righteousness'. Dying to sin includes dying to the kinds of sins we are particularly prone to committing when we are suffering unjustly. Living to righteousness means doing the right thing even in the most difficult situations. That was one of the purposes the Lord had in mind as he endured his sufferings. Another Isaiah 53 quote follows (53:5), to underline that the Saviour's sorrows mark the beginning of a healing process. We can think of the cross as the decisive major surgery, which is followed by a time of recuperation and gradual recovery. Having freed us from the penalty of sin, Christ goes on to help free us from sin's power in our lives. Having declared us righteous by faith, he proceeds to make us more righteous in practice.

Having freed us from the penalty of sin, Christ goes on to help free us from sin's power in our lives.

Suffering with the right shepherd (v. 25)

Thankfully, as well as a sacrificial lamb to deal with our sins, we also have a shepherd to guide us through the process that lies ahead. Our lives had been heading in the wrong direction; we were 'straying' from where we should have been. We followed our own way, rather than that of our wise and caring shepherd (Isa. 53:6). Sheep are like that—curious, but often unthinking. They need someone to keep an eye on them, to keep them out of trouble, and, when necessary, to get them out of trouble. That is why David could say that his shepherd's 'rod and … staff' comforted him (Ps. 23:4). They were the tools for the job of keeping him safe—despite himself. Peter has already warned us that as Christians we have passions that war against our souls (v. 11). Thankfully, we also have a shepherd who is not only looking after our physical needs, but also watching over (the literal meaning of the Greek word translated 'Overseer') our souls. We really can trust him—in our sufferings, and with our spirits. Having been in tremendous danger, and having returned to such a good shepherd, it would be the height of folly to begin to stray once again.

For further study ▶

FOR FURTHER STUDY

1. How many different motivations for persevering can you find in Scripture? Give as many references as you can.
2. Read Psalm 31. How many reasons for trusting God does David give us?
3. Read Psalms 10–11. How does the psalmist comfort himself in the midst of injustice?
4. Read Hebrews 11. How can faith help God's people to endure with patience?
5. What biblical examples can you think of where the Lord uses a disciplinary rod to help one of his erring sheep?

TO THINK ABOUT AND DISCUSS

1. What makes it so hard to 'give way' or 'yield' in an argument?
2. In what circumstances can it be justified to complain about treatment in the workplace, and how should a Christian go about it?
3. How do you think suffering produces endurance (Rom. 5:3)?
4. Why do we find it so difficult to trust God? What thoughts and truths can help us to do so?

8 Marital conduct

(3:1–7)

Peter has already given us some general principles for Christian living when dealing with the Christian's responsibilities as a citizen and as a servant. Now he tells us some of the specifics involved in being a good wife and a good husband. Prepare for a counter-cultural challenge!

The word 'likewise' (v. 1) tells us that some of the principles we have looked at in previous chapters will serve us well in the area of marriage, too. Concern for what is right in God's sight remains essential, as does the important consideration of the quality of our witness. But the New Testament never leaves us with pious platitudes and vague generalities. Peter isn't afraid to be specific, and some of his applications could hardly be more pointed—or challenging!

The principles of subjection and respect that he sets out here should come as no surprise if we have taken in what

Peter has already said in his letter about civil authorities and masters. On the other hand, they could hardly be more surprising to those who get their blueprint for marriage from twenty-first-century Western society. Paul speaks of subjection within marriage in two of his letters (Eph. 5:22 and Col. 3:18—translated 'submission' in the ESV, but it is the same Greek word that Peter uses here). The difference is that Peter makes it clear that this principle applies equally to those who are married to unbelievers.

Winning without words (vv. 1–2)

The aim and hope of a wife who submits to her unbelieving husband is that he might be won over. There are no guarantees, but anecdotal evidence suggests that such a happy outcome is not uncommon. However, even if there is no sign of softening in the husband, the duty remains clear. Paul makes the same point to Christians in Corinth: 'how do you know, wife, whether you will save your husband? Or how do you know, husband, whether you will save your wife?' (1 Cor. 7:16). Paul's point is that you can't know, but it is certainly worth a try! The unbelieving partner may have no time for the word of God, but the Christian spouse can become the instrument God uses in his or her conversion instead.

Purity ('pure conduct', v. 2; the word Peter uses is probably designed to place the emphasis on sexual purity—see 2 Cor. 11:2; Titus 2:5) and respect (literally 'fear' in the sense of deep reverence that results in a fear to displease or disappoint) are the other two attitudes Peter impresses upon wives. The early church father Augustine wrote a prayer about his mother in which he recorded that 'she served her husband as her master, and did all she could to win him for You, speaking to him of You by her conduct, by which You made her beautiful ... Finally when her husband was at the end of his earthly span, she gained him for You.'[1] A submissive, pure, respectful wife is likely to make quite an impact on even the harshest of husbands!

Beauty without bottles (vv. 3–4)

A wife's attitude to her husband is key, but next Peter highlights another area where her attitude will be crucial. A concern with outward appearance can easily become too important. Paul would like there to be a change of focus: from outward to inner beauty. Peter's purpose is not to prohibit 'external adorning',[2] but simply to *prioritize* 'the hidden person of the heart' (v. 4). The time we spend on looking after our heart compared to our appearance will tell us a lot about our priorities.

Here is a beauty that is more than skin deep, one that no bottle can instantly achieve. One argument that Peter uses to back up his call is that inner beauty is 'imperishable' (like the word of God, 1:23), while physical beauty fades. Another motivation is that 'man looks on the outward appearance, but the LORD looks on the heart' (1 Sam. 16:7). And when God sees 'a gentle and quiet spirit', he values it highly (2:4). This is the soil from which submission and respect grow. The word translated 'gentle' here is elsewhere translated 'meek' (Matt. 5:5; see also James 1:21; 3:13) or 'humble' (Matt. 21:5). It describes someone with a readiness to yield, whether to God's will or to the wishes of others—the opposite of asserting our rights. The Greek word was used to describe the tameness of an animal, the soothing properties of a medicine or the gentleness of a breeze. It isn't weakness or a timid temperament. Someone has described it as 'strength under control'. Moses and Jesus were 'meek' (Num. 12:3; Matt. 11:29). Meekness is the opposite of self-will with regard to God and of ill-will with regard to others. It trusts God, loves others, and doesn't worry about self. It's not difficult to see what a positive contribution such an attitude will make to a marriage.

Meekness is the opposite of self-will with regard to God and of ill-will with regard to others.

The contribution that a 'quiet spirit' can make to a happy marriage is easy to appreciate too. The Greek word appears in only one other place in the New Testament, where it is translated 'peaceful' or 'peaceable'. Its literal meaning is 'to keep one's seat' and it speaks of a calmness that isn't easily provoked. The related word 'quietness' is used for silence (see Acts 22:2; 1 Tim. 2:11–12), and the connection isn't hard to see. Those of a quiet spirit are more likely to do a good job of controlling their tongues, and, as a result, keeping the peace. Words spoken in the heat of the moment have done untold damage to many a marriage.

Deference without dread (vv. 5–6)

Peter then stresses that this is not a new approach to marriage, but an old one. He appeals to the example of Sarah. In doing so he makes clear that submission includes obedience (v. 6).

But Sarah's obedience was coupled with a respect which found expression in the way she addressed her husband. There is, no doubt, a cultural element to forms of address and what is appropriate, but the respect Sarah showed in calling her husband 'lord' is clear enough and an example to follow, as Peter makes clear. We don't need to take this example literally, but we are supposed to take it seriously.

When he goes on to warn against fear, it is likely that Peter still has Sarah in mind. The verse in which she refers to Abraham as 'lord' (Gen. 18:12) is followed, just three verses later, by a reference to Sarah being afraid. This instance of fear resulted in a lie, so it looks as if Peter is wanting to commend her good example in showing respect, while at the same time warning against following her bad example of a major failure of courage. The further warning against fear in 3:14 strikes the same note. Paul is dealing with the parallel issue of being subject to the governing authorities when he asks, 'Would you have no fear of the one who is in authority? Then do what is good, and you will receive approval' (Rom. 13:3). Paul's basic message is, 'Do what is right, and you will have no need to fear.' It's a theme running through 1 Peter as well. Even if there are consequences to doing what is right, you can trust that God will either take care of them or of you.

The story is told of somebody who was learning to fly and who was having trouble landing his plane. He needed the help of the control tower. As they radioed their instructions, the inexperienced pilot objected, 'But there's a pole there.' This lack of trust met with the reply, 'You take care of the instructions and we'll take care of the obstructions.' Our responsibility is the same. Perhaps the key verse in the whole of 1 Peter is 4:19: 'let those who suffer according to God's will entrust their souls to a faithful Creator while doing good.'

Intimacy without ignorance (v. 7)

Of course, husbands have a God-given role within marriage, too. Peter begins this section with another 'likewise', suggesting that the particular calling of husbands will involve aspects of submission and respect not dissimilar from those of their wives. In his letters, the apostle Paul makes love the pre-eminent duty of a Christian husband. Peter doesn't mention love, but he clearly assumes that love is the background to the marriage relationship as he concentrates on knowledge and care. In the days when Peter was writing, companionship was often a missing dimension in marriage. Many husbands treated their wives as housekeepers and childbearers, there to comply with their requirements, without giving a thought to what that meant for their spouses. Peter makes clear that a Christian outlook is entirely different. Husbands need to know their wives—not to complain that they are 'always' doing this or that, or to exclaim 'Typical!' when something annoys them, but to give them the support and help they need in the areas where they are most needed.

Consideration

To 'live with your wives in an understanding way' clearly means that husbands should be *considerate* in the truest sense of the word. A husband should consider the needs of his wife. He should understand her challenges and struggles. He should spend time thinking what she would appreciate, and what he might be able to do to help. Such consideration should then lead to action.

Care

A key consideration is that women are 'the weaker vessel'. The husband who grasps this will seek to protect and support his wife. The way to honour her accordingly is to care for her. Generally speaking, women will flourish within a marriage when the husband bears in mind that his wife is like a gift with a label reading, 'Fragile! Handle with care!'

Companionship

While there are significant differences between husband and wife that both come to appreciate in a healthy marriage, what they have in common is far more important than what distinguishes them. In a Christian relationship there is a spiritual equality which transcends the physical, mental and emotional distinctives. The couple are together 'heirs … of the grace of life'. There is a sense of partnership here, as they live their Christian lives together with the same goal in view. The 'your' in the final clause ('your prayers') is plural and so, while it could mean husbands collectively, the likelihood is that Peter expects this partnership to be a prayerful one. He would endorse the old adage, 'The couple that prays together stays together.' The motivation Peter adds is then aimed at both wife and husband. Here Peter probably has in mind Psalm 34, which he will be quoting in just a few verses' time (Ps. 34:15; see also 34:17). The wrong attitude and approach to marriage would leave his readers on the wrong side of Psalm 66:18—'If I had cherished iniquity in my heart, the

Lord would not have listened.' As they do what is right in the context of marriage, though, they can share the psalmist's confidence: 'truly God has listened; he has attended to the voice of my prayer' (Ps. 66:19).

FOR FURTHER STUDY

1. Read Ephesians 5:22–25. How do we know that Paul's ideas aren't specific to the age in which he lived?
2. Read Colossians 3:18–19. What added command does Paul give husbands here? Why do you think it is necessary?
3. Read Matthew 1:19. In what way did Joseph show that he had the potential to be a good husband?

TO THINK ABOUT AND DISCUSS

1. In what subtle ways can a wife show disrespect towards her husband, or undermine his authority?
2. In what practical ways can a wife exhibit meekness in a marriage?
3. What kinds of behaviour in a husband show that he lacks understanding of his wife? What key things does a husband need to understand about his wife?
4. What might be involved in 'showing honour to the woman as the weaker vessel'?

9 Peaceful conduct

(3:8–22)

Not only is there a danger of reacting wrongly to the government, our superiors at work and our spouses, but other Christians can be difficult too. Peace should always be a top priority for the Christian. If we are peaceable, the blessing of peace in our hearts and a conscience that is at peace will often follow.

We don't hear so much of it these days, but 'breach of the peace' is a criminal offence in the UK. It is also a crime in the church of Jesus Christ. The apostle Paul spends a significant part of his epistles seeking to promote peace or re-establish peace among Christians. He doesn't advocate peace at any price—truth and sound doctrine are too valuable to be sacrificed—but it is clearly to be a high priority. Here, Peter supplies us with incentives and Old Testament promises to encourage us, as he spells out this aspect of our calling as Christians.

Be a peace-keeper (vv. 8, 10)

Establishing peace is not our job. Only God can do that—through the blood of Christ and the work of the Holy Spirit. We were, at one time, at enmity with God, but, thankfully, that is now in the past. 'Since we have been justified by faith, we have peace with God through our Lord Jesus Christ' (Rom. 5:1). He is our peace. While Christ's work on the cross is the objective basis of our peace, the work of the Holy Spirit is essential in bringing us to the point of personally appropriating that peace, and then going on to experience it subjectively in our hearts. He draws every Christian to Christ, and in so doing brings them together as they share 'one Lord, one faith, one baptism' (Eph. 4:5). It is not an artificial unity, but a dynamic one of shared life and experience. That's the unity that we are frighteningly good at messing up. Our responsibility is to 'maintain the unity of the Spirit in the bond of peace' (Eph. 4:3). It is easier said than done, because doing it involves 'unity of mind, sympathy, brotherly love, a tender heart, and a humble mind' (1 Peter 3:8). Few of those ingredients are common, and they don't come naturally, either.

- *'Unity of mind'*—thinking the same thing—is not easy to achieve. At the time Peter wrote, the Old Testament and apostolic authority were key to attaining this goal. Now we have the further help of the New Testament, and of gifted Bible preachers, teachers and writers over the centuries whose insights are more accessible (and affordable) today than ever. The word 'heretic' comes from a root meaning 'divisive', and it is an appropriate term because heretics come up with their own ideas, rather than submitting to and explaining what God has revealed. But even with the help of Scripture there are still plenty of problems with interpretation—not because the Scriptures lack clarity, but because our hearts lack purity. Sometimes we don't like the truth; sometimes, because of our background or circumstances, we can't see the truth; and at other times, because of ignorance or laziness, we can't grasp the truth. The alarm bells ought to start ringing, though, if we find that our take on the truth lacks the support of those committed to the authority of the Bible over the centuries.

- *'Sympathy'*—feeling the same thing—is something that we can, and must, work on. It involves the ability to put ourselves in the place of others to understand how they see things and how they must feel. We'll need to be careful to recognize that none of us are exactly the same, and so we will want to make allowances for different temperaments, personalities and backgrounds. Listening hard to other people explaining their perspective and sharing their feelings will help us. We have the blessing of a Saviour and High Priest whose sympathy is based on a perfect knowledge of us and our situation. Our goal must be to understand the difficulties others face as well as possible.
- *'Brotherly love'* and *'a tender heart'* both speak of the impact that our knowledge of others should have on us. It's no good being able to assess accurately what

someone else is going through if we don't care. Again, our Saviour is the perfect role model. We might combine the two under the heading *'sensitivity'*. The more concerned we are for the welfare of others, and the more we share in their pain and sorrow, happiness and joy, the closer we are to Jesus' example. As Paul put it, we are to 'rejoice with those who rejoice' and to 'weep with those who weep' (Rom. 12:15). If we struggle to be glad for those who are knowing blessings of one sort or another, the likelihood is that we will also struggle to sympathize with and support others through tough times. Putting others first doesn't come easily, but it's what is needed.

- Of necessity that will mean putting ourselves last, and for that we will need *'a humble mind'*. Self-importance is a characteristic of pride; placing importance on others is a feature of humility. Pride breeds conflict because it is competitive in nature; humility promotes peace because the humble person is always ready to waive his or her rights, rather than insist upon them. Some people thrive on conflict, but that should not be true of the Christian.

Humility promotes peace because the humble person is always ready to waive his or her rights, rather than insist upon them.

Words spoken in haste are often the source of conflict. Often it is a quick retort or barbed comment that disturbs the peace of a Christian fellowship. That's why it is so important to watch our tongues. Evil words (v. 10) easily escape if we are not on our guard, but misleading words are a danger too. While unkind words can lead to hostility, deceitful words can lead to a kind of 'cold war' of mutual distrust, involving manoeuvring and manipulation. A wayward tongue will upset others, but it makes trouble for ourselves too.

Be a peace-seeker (vv. 9, 11–12)

Peace-keeping is largely negative in its focus—seeking to avoid actions, words and attitudes that might cause conflict. Peace-seeking, though, has a much more positive thrust. Peter's teaching includes 'not 'repay[ing]', but goes well beyond it. There is something to do 'on the contrary' (v. 9), and that something is to 'bless'. Instead of calling down a curse on our enemies, we should pray for them and desire their blessing. 'May it not be charged against them!' is a prayer we can pray along with Paul (2 Tim. 4:16). Again, a motivating promise is attached: if we seek the blessing of others we will, in the process, 'obtain a blessing' for ourselves. Peter may well be thinking of Psalm 133, where we are told that a place of unity is the place where 'the LORD has commanded the blessing' (Ps. 133:3). That's a good place to be!

To actively promote peace means to go that extra mile. Paul was realistic when he encouraged the Christians at Rome to seek peace 'so far as it depends on you' (Rom. 12:18). There is only so much we can do, but we must do what we can.

Be a peace-owner … (vv. 13–14)

Again Peter laces his exhortations with promises. Righteous

conduct in this area of peace-maintenance will be seen in heaven, and that ensures that our prayers will be heard there too. Evildoers enjoy no such privilege (Ps. 66:18). Being 'zealous for what is good' (v. 13) doesn't generally make enemies, but even if it does we can be assured of God's blessing in the long run (v. 14). We may, like the farmer, have to wait, but James assures us that 'a harvest of righteousness is sown in peace by those who make peace' (James 3:18).

… in your heart (v. 15)

Even if, in the short term, we may not be able to enjoy peace with others, we can know peace within. Fear and disturbance need not have a place in our hearts as long as Christ is honoured there (v. 15). Peter is quoting the prophet Isaiah (Isa. 8:12–13), who was being warned not to give way to fear of the surrounding nations. Instead he was to fear (in the sense of deep reverence) 'the LORD of hosts'. Peter has seen the parallel with his day, and the prospect of persecution: 'Don't worry; just honour Christ and be prepared to answer the questions of your persecutors appropriately. In the long run "you will be blessed".' You will be able to say with the psalmist, 'Return, O my soul, to your rest' (Ps. 116:7).

… in your conscience (vv. 16–22)

Not only is there peace in the heart to be enjoyed, but there is also a peaceful conscience (v. 16). The preciousness of that is really only appreciated by those who know what it is like to have a troubled, accusing conscience. We are given three contributing factors to a clear conscience:

The gentleness and respect of their testimony (vv. 16–17)

As these Christians 'make a defence' (v. 15) they need to be careful. Peter sees another way in which suffering could come as a result of our own foolishness. It's not easy to speak boldly when put on the spot (as Peter knew all too well—see Matt. 26:69–75), but, if we manage to, it can be just as difficult to do so with 'gentleness and respect' (v. 16). Peter is probably thinking of a formal trial, though the principle applies equally to personal conversation. It isn't just a matter of what we say, but how we say it. You can win the argument, but lose the person, so a winning manner is just as important as winning the debate. What makes it even more important is that such an attitude will leave your conscience clear, while at the same time convicting the consciences of your detractors. You will be able to say, 'I have nothing to be ashamed of; I spoke with gentleness and respect', while those who slander you will be 'put to shame'. In circumstances like this, suffering is 'God's will' (v. 17). We are simply following in the footsteps of our Saviour, as he warned we might have to.

You can win the argument, but lose the person, so a winning manner is just as important as winning the debate.

The death and resurrection of Christ (v. 18)

His suffering has secured a clear conscience for us, because it was 'for sins' (v. 18). That his sacrifice was accepted and our sin has been dealt with is shown by the resurrection, when he was 'made alive in the spirit'.

> I will trust in the cross of my Redeemer,
> I will sing of the blood that never fails;
> Of sins forgiven, of conscience cleansed,
> Of death defeated and life without end.[1]

The symbolism of the flood and baptism (vv. 19–22)

Peter sees another parallel here: between the floodwaters of Noah's day and the waters of baptism. What links the two is Jesus' proclamation 'to the spirits in prison' (v. 19). Quite how it links the two is not easy to understand. Peter's thought here is complicated, the Greek isn't easy, and the lack of any parallel passages in the New Testament makes any firm conclusion difficult. He could be referring to Noah's preaching as the flood approached, which was delivered with the help of Christ, by the Spirit, to people who are now spirits in prison.[2] Even if we are mistaken about Peter's meaning here, the main point is that Noah and his family's being 'brought safely through water' (v. 20) is a picture (or type[3]) of baptism. All Christians who have obediently gone 'safely through water' have a cleansed conscience. They emerge from the water to 'newness of life' (Rom. 6:4). By virtue of their union with Christ they can be spoken of as seated with him at the right hand of the Father, and one day they will reign with him in his everlasting kingdom.

For further study ▶

FOR FURTHER STUDY

1. What were the chief causes of disunity in the churches of the New Testament? What are the chief causes today?
2. Read Romans 12:14–21. What are the contributing factors to disharmony described here, and how do they lead to it?
3. Read Proverbs 10:19; 12:18; 13:3; 15:2, 4; 16:24; 21:23; 25:15; 31:26. What can we learn about our words from these verses?
4. Read Psalm 133. What do the two pictures in this psalm teach us about the kind of blessing that unity brings?
5. Read Acts 23:1–5; 24:1–21; 26:25–29. In what ways did Paul show respect in these speeches? Was there any lack of respect, and if so, why?

TO THINK ABOUT AND DISCUSS

1. How do we go about distinguishing between what it is essential to be united about and what it's OK to disagree about?
2. What steps can we take that can help us become more sympathetic to others?
3. When have you been hurt by words or hurt someone else with your own words?
4. When was the last time your conscience troubled you? What did you do about it? Can you think back to a time when your conscience powerfully convicted you about something that many might consider a fairly minor matter?

10 Right-minded conduct

(4:1–11)

Christianity is not just a way of life, it's a way of thinking. Think right, and heart and will often follow with relative ease. To keep thinking right, we'll need to be ready for some of the things that can lead our thoughts astray, and to keep some key thoughts at the forefront of our minds.

A ready mind (v. 1)

A big part of the good fight of faith is the battle for the mind, and Peter wants us to be well armed. A number of times in the New Testament we are told that, as we set about living the Christian life, a vital truth to grasp is that when we believe in the Lord Jesus Christ we are united to him (Rom. 6:5). That means that in an important sense we died with Christ (Rom. 6:8; 2 Cor. 5:14; 2 Tim. 2:11). We also rose with him and are seated with him in heavenly places (Eph. 2:6; Col. 2:12; 3:1), but it is the dying with Christ (sometimes referred to as our having been crucified with Christ) that Peter is concerned with here. It has implications for our daily living, and, as Peter points out, for our daily thinking. He wants his readers to be fore-armed—ready for anything. They need 'to get their head straight', as we might put it. And that is what the Scriptures are for: they show us what it means to see things clearly; to know what is most important; to have an eternal perspective on things. That's not so easy in the heat of the moment when we are under pressure or being tempted. Our minds need to be trained. In the army, training exercises and drills are all designed to ensure that, in the heat of battle, in the thick of the fight, the right reaction is instinctive. That needs to be our aim in the Christian life.

- In Rome the Christians were told that they needed to be 'transformed by the renewal of [their] mind' (Rom. 12:2).
- In Corinth they were told to 'look not to the things that are seen but to the things that are unseen' (2 Cor. 4:18).
- In Ephesus they needed to be 'renewed in the spirit of [their] minds' (Eph. 4:23).
- In Philippi they were to 'have this mind ... which [was theirs] in Christ Jesus' (Phil. 2:5).
- In Colossae believers were instructed to 'set [their] minds on things that are above, not on things that are on earth' (Col. 3:2).

It's interesting to see that modern psychology has begun to recognize the importance of our mindset/worldview with the relatively recent development of cognitive therapy. The Bible offers the best cognitive therapy of all.

Ready for God's will (vv. 2–3)

The kind of thinking Peter wants us to do is the same as that advocated by Paul in his letter to the Christians in Rome. Christ's death was decisive and marked the end of his sin-bearing work. Christians should see their conversion as marking a similarly decisive break with sin in their lives. Paul talks about 'reckoning' in Romans 6, while Peter talks about being armed with the right way of thinking, but it amounts to the same thing. Here are the sorts of thoughts Peter wants us to have:

- 'Christ has finished with sin; I'm supposed to be finished with sin too' (see 4:1).
- 'Christ was put to death in the flesh but made alive in the spirit; I used to live in the flesh but now I'm to live in the spirit' (see 3:18).
- 'I used to live for human passions, but now I am to live for the will of God' (see 4:2).
- 'I've spent more than enough time doing what *I* want to do; from now on I only want to do what God wants me to do' (see 4:2–3).

It's not a bad idea for us to stop every now and then and ask ourselves what we 'live for' (v. 2). Some people live for pleasure or excitement; for others it might be a hobby or an indulgence. It's possible to 'live for the weekend' or the next holiday. Even our families can become an idol, whether it's wives, husbands, children or grandchildren. We probably all know people who 'come alive' when talking about a particular topic. For the Christian, that topic should be God's will. We're supposed to mean it when we pray 'Thy will be done'. And we should be able to add 'not mine' with equal enthusiasm.

All those who journey, soon or late,
Must pass within the garden's gate;
Must kneel alone in darkness there,
And battle with some fierce despair.
God pity those who cannot say,
'Not mine but thine', who only pray,
'Let this cup pass', and cannot see
The *purpose* of Gethsemane.[1]

The apostle Paul's words should be ours too: 'What shall I do, Lord?' (Acts 22:10). It's a question we can ask with confidence rather than trepidation. The Lord's will for us will be perfectly in keeping with his grace, mercy and love, however inclined we are to doubt it. His will really will be better than ours, even if our sinful nature tries to convince us otherwise. In Romans, Paul challenges the Christians there as to where following their own wills had got them and would get them (Rom. 6:21). 'Doing our own thing' will often give us much to be ashamed of, and if we never alter course, Paul tells us, it will lead to death. The healthy Christian, on the other hand, longs for holiness and, ultimately, eternal life (6:22).

Peter spells out what kinds of sin he has in mind, associated with 'the flesh', 'human passions' and 'the Gentiles'. Sex and drink are the areas of temptation he highlights (v. 3). 'Lawless idolatry' is probably added to the list because of the close links between many of the rituals and ceremonies of idolatrous paganism, and prostitution and excessive drinking. Paganism may not have the influence it once had, but atheism worships at the shrines of sex and drink too.

Ready for opposition (vv. 4–6)

The radical change of lifestyle that comes from such a different way of thinking isn't, however, likely to be welcomed by those who continue to indulge themselves. Sinners like company, and they don't understand why some will not join in (v. 4). What could be the motivation for denying oneself something pleasurable? They generally resent those who disapprove, and that resentment often leads to slander. The early church faced accusations of cannibalism and incest because of a misunderstanding of their 'love feasts' (as the Lord's Supper was known). Such slanderers will one day be called to account (v. 5). In fact, all will be judged—'the living and the dead' covers everyone! Unbelievers who die before Christ's return won't escape, and believers who have died will not miss out on eternal life. The gospel was preached to them while they were alive (v. 6), and their salvation (a spiritual one until their resurrection) will one day be complete. Just as the godless will ultimately be judged, so those they have wrongly condemned (and it looks as if Peter is talking about martyrdom here) will ultimately be vindicated. Earthly, temporal judgement (and even death) will be succeeded by heavenly, spiritual vindication and everlasting life.

Sinners like company, and they don't understand why some will not join in.

Ready for the end of all things (v. 7)

His readers' detractors were behaving as they liked with no

sense of accountability. In his second letter Peter gives us a glimpse of their way of thinking: 'Where is the promise of his coming? For ever since the fathers fell asleep, all things are continuing as they were from the beginning of creation' (2 Peter 3:4). The Christian, in contrast, knows that 'the end of all things is at hand' (1 Peter 4:7). That should have a profound impact on our lives.

First, we will be motivated to control ourselves, rather than giving in to our passions. If there is no 'end of all things', the maxim 'Eat, drink and be merry' makes a lot of sense. But knowing that we will have to give an account of our lives means that every little indulgence will come back to haunt us.

Second, by now it will come as no surprise that 'the end of all things' should also dramatically influence the way we think. We will be 'sober-minded'. The Greek literally means 'safe in mind' (see its use in Mark 5:15; Luke 8:35) and indicates that we will have our thoughts under control, aware of the solemn day of judgement towards which we are heading. Getting this right will not only make a difference on the last day, though: it will also give potency to our prayers. As our lives are characterized by righteousness, the effectiveness of our prayers will increase, as James also tells us in his letter (James 5:16).

Ready to serve in the meantime (vv. 8–11)

So every detail of our lives matters in the here and now, while the big picture helps us to see what our priorities need to be. In light of the fast-approaching end of all things, loving service is what we need to concentrate on. There should be no slackening off. We need to '*keep* loving one another' (v. 8).

And there needs to be a real intensity and sincerity to that love: we need to love 'earnestly'. One of the wonderful things about love is that it 'covers a multitude of sins', and the sad fact is that among a fellowship of sinners there will be a multitude that needs covering. There is a wicked kind of delight that our sinful nature can derive from the falls of others. That's something we need to be on the lookout for, because it is usually connected to a feeding of our egos, and exhibits a lack of the love Peter expects to find among Christians.

That love should find expression in service. Whether it is our homes or our gifts, we will want to use them to bless our brothers and sisters in Christ (vv. 8–9). They are gracious gifts from God that we cannot keep for ourselves; they are committed to us, their 'stewards' (v. 10). Our gracious God is the one who gives us not only the gifts, but also the strength with which to put them to good use (v. 11).

Peter closes this section of his letter with a timely reminder of our aim as we serve one another in love. We aren't doing it to be popular or to feel good about ourselves. We want God to be glorified. We want others to look at our lives and recognize that anything praiseworthy about them is God's work. We want him to get the credit (v. 11).

The American actor Kevin Bacon tells of how his young son was impressed after seeing his father's role in the 1984 dance film *Footloose*. He asked, 'Dad, you know that thing in the movie where you swing from the rafters of that building? That's really cool, how did you do that?' Bacon had to explain that a stunt man had done that bit. A second question followed about another part of the film, but again Bacon had to explain that it too had been done by someone else. It was followed by a rather disappointed, 'Dad, what *did* you do?', to which came the answer, 'I got all the glory.'[2]

We must make sure that *God* gets all the glory. He is worthy to be praised. We aren't.

FOR FURTHER STUDY

1. Read Genesis 19:4–9 and Exodus 2:11–14. What lay at the root of the hostility in these passages?
2. Read Luke 12:13–21. In what way was this parable a response to the man in the crowd? What mistakes had the rich man made?
3. Read Ecclesiastes 2:18–26 and 5:8–6:2. How does the philosophy here differ from that of the rich man in the parable?
4. What biblical examples can you find of people keeping glory for themselves, instead of acknowledging their dependence on God?
5. Read Romans 12:3–8. What sort of sober-mindedness is Paul talking about here?

TO THINK ABOUT AND DISCUSS

1. What would you say to someone whose philosophy of life amounted to 'Eat, drink and be merry'?
2. What will help you to be 'transformed by the renewal of your mind' (Rom. 12:2)?
3. What sorts of things might Christians worry about concerning God's will for them, and how would you deal with those anxieties?

11 Believing conduct

(4:12–19)

If we are thinking straight as Christians, trials will come as no surprise. What may surprise us is Peter's prescription for meeting them. Our need? Joy and trust. Our aim? To glorify God.

Peter addresses his readers affectionately (v. 12). He knows that they are approaching testing times, and he genuinely wants to help. And the best way to help them is to prepare them for it. They mustn't be taken unawares. Our initial reaction when a tough trial comes our way will depend on our theology. If we've fallen for some form (however subtle) of prosperity gospel, then suffering will perplex us and be considered 'strange' (v. 12). If, however, we've read, registered and digested what the Bible (and this letter in particular) has to say about tribulations, then we'll be ready.

Don't be surprised (v. 12)

Don't be surprised when trials come

Trials are part and parcel of the Christian life. The Bible

tells us so. Jesus said so (John 15:20). Paul tells us that it is through 'many tribulations' that we must 'enter the kingdom of God' (Acts 14:22). Peter speaks in this letter of 'various trials' (1 Peter 1:6). Trials *will* come, and we need to be ready for them.

Don't be surprised at their intensity

Peter speaks here about 'the fiery trial' that his readers will have to face, suggesting a specific period of persecution. The word 'fiery' makes clear that a particularly intense trial is on the way. Some tests are short and sweet, but Peter is talking about a thorough examination. The use of the word 'fiery' may be intended to turn our thoughts to Shadrach, Meshach and Abednego (Dan. 3:8–30) and the possibility of martyrdom. Those three men were neither surprised nor daunted. The calmness with which they answered the king speaks volumes:

> O Nebuchadnezzar, we have no need to answer you in this matter. If this be so [that we are to be cast into the furnace], our God whom we serve is able to deliver us from the burning fiery furnace, and he will deliver us out of your hand, O king. But if not, be it known to you, O king, that we will not serve your gods or worship the golden image that you have set up (Dan. 3:16–18).

Roughly two thousand years later two other men, Nicholas Ridley and Hugh Latimer, were facing a similar fate. As they arrived at the stake where they were to be burned Ridley embraced Latimer and said, 'Be of good heart, brother, for God will either assuage the fury of the flame, or else strengthen us to abide it.' As the stake was lit Latimer in turn said, 'Be of good cheer, Ridley; and play the man. We shall this day, by God's grace, light up such a candle in England, as I trust, will never be put out.' We are then told,

> When Dr. Ridley saw the fire flaming up towards him, he cried with a wonderful loud voice, 'Lord, Lord, receive my spirit.' Master Latimer, crying as vehemently on the other side, 'O Father of heaven, receive my soul!' received the flame as it were embracing of it. After that he had stroked his face with his hands, and as it were, bathed them a little in the fire, he soon died (as it appeareth) with very little pain or none.[1]

Most Christians find that the difficulties and challenges of everyday life, while testing in a number of ways, don't greatly shake their faith. Traumas and tragedies are a different matter. Peter wants it to be said of us, 'He is not afraid of bad news; his heart is firm, trusting in the LORD' (Ps. 112:7). When it comes to coping with really tough news or situations, our starting point is to recognize that this is nothing strange. Our Lord never promised us an easy, stress-free life. In fact, quite the opposite.

When it comes to coping with really tough news or situations, our starting point is to recognize that this is nothing strange.

I recently heard an interview with a golfer in the European Ryder Cup team who was saying how, when things seemed to be going against them on the morning of the competition's final day, they were ready for it, because they'd talked about it the evening before. What could have shaken their confidence and led to mistakes and low morale didn't, because they had anticipated the situation. Peter wants us to be similarly prepared. If we aren't in the midst of trials right now, we should be praying and preparing for the time when we will be. And that may be sooner than we think …

Don't be surprised at their purpose

Peter also wants us to understand the purpose these trials serve in the Christian life. Fiery trials come to 'test' us, Peter says. The saying is so popular that it may have lost its force, but it is true nonetheless: 'These things are sent to try us.' Back in chapter 1 Peter has already pointed out that trials test the genuineness of our faith (1:6–7), but they can also call true faith into exercise, serving to refine and strengthen it. Again, in chapter 1 Peter has already mentioned the refining, purifying effect of trials (1:6–7). Passing metals through fire to purify them would have been familiar to his readers, and the use of the term 'fiery' (4:12) makes that connection. Just as tests we took at school were designed to cement in our minds things we had already learned, so tests in the Christian life can serve to hammer home lessons that we otherwise might fail to grasp.

Paul gives us further reasons for why we can 'rejoice in our sufferings' in his letter to the Christians in Rome (Rom. 5:2–5): they help to build our stamina (or 'endurance'; the Greek word means 'staying power'), strengthen character (the Greek word means 'tried-and-tested'-ness), and enliven hope (see also James 1:3–4). But a trial doesn't accomplish these things automatically: we will need the right attitude if we are to be 'trained by it' (Heb. 12:11). The first step is to appreciate what God's purpose in the trial might be.

When you know some of the wonderful things that God can accomplish through trials, you can look at them as heaven-sent opportunities for growth.

Do rejoice (vv. 13–14)

Do rejoice that your sufferings bring you closer to Christ

Scripture often begins with the negative before moving on to the positive, and Peter does that here. If we are not to be surprised by trials, we are (surprisingly!) to rejoice! It sounds like a tall order, but then Peter goes on to explain that there is a real sense in which we are sharing Christ's sufferings. Paul puts the same thought in a different way to the Colossians when, speaking of his own sufferings, he says that he is 'filling up what is lacking in Christ's afflictions' (Col. 1:24). He talks to the Philippians, too, about how he longed to know Christ 'and the power of his resurrection, and ... share his sufferings' (Phil. 3:10). This is a 'fellowship of suffering' which brings us closer to Christ and makes him increasingly precious to us.

Do rejoice that your sufferings will one day be succeeded by glory

Peter also makes the point that sufferings should fill us with hope, as we think of the glory that lies ahead. One day Jesus' glory will be revealed, and it is well worth thinking about that during testing times (v. 13). The day is coming when there will be no more suffering (Rev. 21:4), and the end of suffering will be followed by endless glory. This is how hope develops through exercise. It's not the first time that Peter has stressed the order: suffering first, *then* glory.

Do rejoice that your sufferings will be accompanied by help from the Holy Spirit

And then there is the sustaining work of the Holy Spirit (v. 14). Those who are being insulted and persecuted 'for the name of Christ' will know more of his presence and strength than others do. Jesus made this point when speaking to his disciples (Matt. 10:16–20; Luke 12:11–12). Now that is a blessing to rejoice about!

Don't be ashamed (vv. 15–16)

Of course, there is a brand of suffering that brings none of these blessings in its wake. Peter has given us a number of ways of looking at the right kind of suffering. We are to suffer:

- 'as servants of God' (2:16);
- 'for righteousness' sake' (3:14);
- 'for the name of Christ' (4:14);
- 'as a Christian' (4:16);
- 'according to God's will' (4:19).

But we need to make sure that our suffering isn't the wrong kind: 'as a murderer or a thief or an evildoer or as a meddler' (4:15). The first three terms are self-explanatory, but the final one may well be designed to give us pause for thought. 'Meddlers', according to the Greek word used here, are those who interfere in things that are not really their responsibility. It could have been translated 'troublemaker'. Paul uses a similar word in 2 Thessalonians and 1 Timothy which is translated 'busybodies' (see especially 2 Thes. 3:11). They are just the kind of people to put people's backs up because of their interfering, only to then complain about persecution when their contribution isn't welcomed.

If any of these four labels belong to us we have every reason to be ashamed, Peter says. But we are not to be ashamed if we have been doing good as a Christian, whatever kind of persecution we have to endure (v. 16). Although the name 'Christian' seems originally to have been used as a term of abuse (in Antioch; see Acts 11:26), it is a name to be thankful for (1 Peter 4:16). Suffering for our Saviour's sake, bearing his name, is the right kind of suffering—the kind that brings glory to God.

Do trust (vv. 17–19)

Next, Peter encourages his readers to trust God, even as a period of persecution is approaching. This is a familiar pattern from the Old Testament. The people of God were often invaded, besieged and even carried off into captivity, as Israel's prophets had warned would happen. But with the message of imminent judgement often came a message of encouragement. Beyond the judgement a remnant would flourish, and in due course the persecutors would face God's judgement themselves. That same cycle is going to be repeated again, says Peter. Judgement is to begin with the household of God, but worse awaits their enemies (v. 17). While God's people might only just survive, the ungodly face punishment without hope. Patient endurance is what is needed as they trust in God's assurances that justice will ultimately be done. 'Hang on!' is the message.

But this is not to be a hanging-on in desperation tinged with panic. 'Entrusting' (v. 19) is something to be done calmly, and

Peter tells us the source of such calmness and peace: we have a 'faithful Creator'. No one whose hope is in him will ever be put to shame (Ps. 22:5; 25:3). He is the guardian of our souls. Persecutors may be able to harm us or even take our lives, but, as the Lord Jesus said, it is only our bodies they can harm; they cannot touch the soul (Matt. 10:28). This 'entrusting' is not to be merely passive, though: it is to be accompanied by 'doing good'. This is one of Peter's themes (see 2:12, 14–15, 20; 3:6, 11, 13, 16–17; 4:19). We can sum up his teaching here with the familiar advice issued during the Second World War: 'KEEP CALM & CARRY ON.' Or we could use another well-known phrase: 'TRUST AND OBEY!'

For further study ▶

FOR FURTHER STUDY

1. Find out what kinds of fiery trials Christians are facing in different parts of the world today.
2. Read 2 Corinthians 12:7–10. What was the Lord's purpose in allowing Paul to suffer? How did the thorn in the flesh help achieve it?
3. Read John 9:1–7. What is the reason Jesus gives for this man's suffering? What would you say to someone who thought that it was an unsatisfactory explanation?
4. Read Luke 24:25–27. What passages in the Old Testament do you think the Lord might have referred to here?
5. Read Ezekiel 9:3–10. Why do you think Peter refers to this passage at this point (v. 17) in his letter? Are there any parallels?

TO THINK ABOUT AND DISCUSS

1. How would you explain what the 'prosperity gospel' is in its extreme form? What does it look like in its more subtle forms?
2. In what ways might the Holy Spirit help us in times of suffering?
3. How does God use suffering for good in the Christian life, and how can we ensure that we fully benefit from such times?

12 Needful conduct

(5:1–14)

As 'the fiery trial' approaches, Peter is acutely aware of what the church will need to see it through: shepherds who are ready and willing to lead, along with humble sheep ready and willing to follow. A firm reliance upon God combined with equally firm resistance to the devil will enable them to emerge on the other side, owing everything to 'the God of all grace'.

The good Shepherd loves his sheep, and one aspect of his care for them is the provision of under-shepherds. Peter himself had received the commission to feed Christ's sheep and now he wants to encourage others fulfilling the same role. He addresses them as colleagues (v. 1), while gently reminding them of his apostolic credentials as a 'witness of the sufferings of Christ'. He had been in Gethsemane, and in the courtyard of the high priest (Mark 14:54). He had also, of course, witnessed a revelation of Christ's glory on the mount of transfiguration (Matt. 17:1–8). But that was only a foretaste of the glory yet to be revealed, in which they would all one day share.

The need for guidance (vv. 2–4)

In the meantime, though, God's flock needs shepherding (v. 2), which means that local churches need elders. The role is one that calls for vigilance because they are to be 'exercising oversight'—all the more so because there are cunning wolves around (disguised as sheep! Matt. 7:15), as well as a lion who is on the prowl (v. 8). And those elders need to be willing; it is a role that they should have some desire to fill. It shouldn't be a matter of somebody dolefully 'doing their duty'. Paul mentions this to Timothy as he begins to set out the qualities an overseer[1] must have (1 Tim. 3:1). Cheerful service is the goal; it always has been ('serve the LORD with … gladness', Deut. 28:47). The Lord seeks willing workers—and so do local churches. This willingness should spring from a desire to serve, and emphatically not from the desire to earn (v. 2). To be motivated by money while serving in this way is to miss the point entirely.

Others may not struggle with money so much as the power that such a position confers. The eldership is no place for power-hungry control freaks. 'Domineering' (v. 3) is out. The power that elders can wield most safely is that of a good example. Seeking a reward in the here and now would be a big mistake, but looking forward to an 'unfading crown of glory' (v. 4) will help no end. The chief Shepherd is returning, and rewarding faithful under-shepherds will be high on the agenda when he does.

The need for compliance (vv. 5–6)

Peter now addresses those who are not elders in the church. It's that verb 'subject' again (v. 5; we met it in 2:13, 18; 3:1). The church needs those who will lead, but it also needs those who will follow. If you aren't a leader, you need to focus on being a good follower. Many a church has suffered when those who are called to follow have tried to lead. Others have struggled when elders have failed to lead and a kind of democracy (that the Bible knows nothing of) has prevailed.

> If you aren't a leader, you need to focus on being a good follower.

Elders do have an authority that needs to be not only acknowledged but also submitted to. The principle of respect that we have seen applied in other areas is applicable here too, as Hebrews makes clear (Heb. 13:17). Church life is at its best when elders lead in humility and the flock humbly follow their lead. That is what Peter is encouraging when he calls on all Christians to 'clothe' themselves 'with humility towards one another'. Peter is probably thinking of his experience in the upper room, watching Jesus 'clothe himself' with a towel as an example of humble leadership (John 13:3–5). That is the ideal example. The nightmare scenario is the one where pride reigns. Proud elders think they know best and lay down the law without carefully consulting Scripture or taking into account the views and feelings of those under their charge. Proud church members resent and resist the authority of their overseers, convinced that they could run the church better, even though God has not called them to do so. The worst thing about this state of affairs, though, is that such a fellowship will find that God is opposed to them (v. 5). In contrast, there is wonderful encouragement to those who do manage to 'clothe [them]selves ... with humility': they can expect to receive 'grace' from God.

A standard definition of 'grace' is 'free, undeserved favour', but in this context the emphasis is on favour in the form of 'the help that is needed'. If you want to experience God's help in your life, humility is a must. After all, without humility we won't even admit our need of help, never mind receive it. Peter seems then to move on to a slightly different area of humility, when he mentions humbling ourselves 'under the mighty hand of God' (v. 6). Here it sounds like a submission to, and acceptance of, our situation in providence. Implicit in that surrender is a recognition that our circumstances are ordered by God. Instead of exalting ourselves, we need to leave that to God and his timing. God's time is always 'the proper time'.

The need for reliance (v. 7)

The temptation in difficulties is to become anxious about the outcome and to conclude that God doesn't care. But to do so is to distrust the Lord and to call him a liar. On the contrary, we can leave our anxieties with him, confident in the knowledge that he really does care, regardless of how we feel or think (v. 7).

Frank Graeff (1860–1919) was known as 'the sunshine minister' because of his optimistic attitude and sunny disposition. Nevertheless, he knew times of great despondency, doubt and pain. It was after just such a period that he wrote a hymn containing the following words:

Does Jesus care when my heart is pained
Too deeply for mirth and song;
As the burdens press, and the cares distress,
And the way grows weary and long?
Does Jesus care when my way is dark
With a nameless dread and fear?
As the daylight fades into deep night shades,
Does He care enough to be near?
Oh yes, He cares—I know He cares!
His heart is touched with my grief;
When the days are weary,
The long nights dreary,
I know my Saviour cares.

We are all troubled by anxieties at times, but what matters is what we *do* with them. They need to be 'cast' on the Lord. This isn't a passive letting go of worry, but an active handing it over to the Lord. We give it to him.

The story is told of a businessman who was plagued by anxiety. He had tried all sorts of things but just couldn't stop fretting. In the end he placed an advert offering a handsome wage to someone whose job it would be to do his worrying for him. He interviewed a number of candidates until finally he was convinced that he had found his man. As they shook hands to confirm the appointment the new employee said that he had just one question: 'How on earth are you going to afford my salary?' 'That's your concern now, not mine,' came the reply.

We are to let the Lord do our worrying for us. Peter

probably had in mind these words of David, who urged, 'Cast your burden on the LORD, and he will sustain you; he will never permit the righteous to be moved' (Ps. 55:22).

The Greek word Peter uses here has the literal meaning 'to throw upon'. It is used in only one other place in the New Testament—to describe the disciples 'throwing their cloaks on the colt' as Jesus prepared to enter Jerusalem (Luke 19:35). 'Don't carry your worries around yourself; let the Lord do the donkey work' is Peter's advice. There is a prayer used by the hill people of Haiti that conveys the same idea: 'Lord, don't let us put our load of trouble in a basket on our head. Help us put them on Jesus' head. Then we won't have headaches.' Amen to that!

'Don't carry your worries around yourself; let the Lord do the donkey work' is Peter's advice.

The need for vigilance (v. 8)

We haven't finished once we've got the better of anxieties. Yes, the Father cares for us, but we have an enemy who doesn't care for us at all. The devil is out to get us, and he is a formidable foe. He is no harmless figure of fun, but a Moriarty-like criminal mastermind. We will need to be 'sober-minded' and 'watchful' if he is not to get the better of us. He combines the subtlety of a serpent with the ferocity of a lion, and our destruction is his goal. Peter knew that all too well. The Lord had told Peter of the need for vigilance in Gethsemane, but 'watching' was what Peter singularly failed to do (Matt. 26:38–41). He underestimated the power of the devil, to his cost. We need to be careful not to make the same mistake.

The need for resistance (v. 9)

'Resistance is futile' was the slogan of the Borgs in *Star Trek*. Thankfully, the opposite is true, according to Scripture. We are assured that, if we remain resolute in our resistance, the devil will flee from us (James 4:7). He tries to convince us that the Borgs are right and that we have no alternative but to give in to his temptation this time. Peter and James, however, combine to tell us that nothing could be further from the truth. We know that he seeks to undermine faith (Luke 22:31–32), so that is where we must remain firm. God's promises are true whatever the devil, the world around us or even sin within us might say. We can hold on to many precious promises to sustain us in our spiritual warfare:

- 'He who is in you is greater than he who is in the world' (1 John 4:4).
- 'With the temptation [God] will also provide the way of escape, that you may be able to endure it' (1 Cor. 10:13).
- 'Sin will have no dominion over you' (Rom. 6:14).

Our conviction that these statements are true can't afford to waver. But help is at hand.

As we stand firm we can encourage ourselves with the thought that we are standing together (5:9). Many other Christians around the world are fighting the same battles as us. We need to hang on. The Duke of Wellington is supposed to have said that the British soldiers at the Battle of Waterloo weren't braver than Napoleon's soldiers, they were just brave for five minutes longer—and that made the difference between victory and defeat. We all need to 'withstand in the evil day, and having done all, to stand firm' (Eph. 6:13).

The need for perseverance (vv. 10–14)

Not only is help at hand, but there is eternal glory ahead. While suffering is inevitable and can be acute and sustained, it will not last for ever: there will be an end to it. We have another set of promises that our faith needs to hold onto here:

- 'The sufferings of this present time are not worth comparing with the glory that is to be revealed to us' (Rom. 8:18).
- 'This light momentary affliction is preparing for us an eternal weight of glory beyond all comparison' (2 Cor. 4:17).
- 'We know that when he appears we shall be like him, because we shall see him as he is' (1 John 3:2).
- 'He will wipe away every tear from their eyes, and death shall be no more, neither shall there be mourning, nor crying, nor pain any more, for the former things have passed away' (Rev. 21:4).

Even if we do falter, we have a God who will pick us up and help us on our way again. Peter knew what it was like to be mauled by the roaring lion he's been talking about. But he also knew all about being restored (or repaired), confirmed, strengthened and established (v. 10; see John 21:15–17).

'The true grace of God' (v. 12) has been Peter's theme. He has just repeated the promise with which he opened his letter: that 'a little while' (1:6; 5:10) of suffering will ultimately give place to glory—and that's all because of God's grace. It's a promise we need to remain confident about. Only then will we be able to endure suffering with a faith that passes all tests, while at the same time enjoying a peace that passes all understanding.

For further study ▶

FOR FURTHER STUDY

1. Read Ezekiel 34:1–6. What are the chief characteristics of these bad shepherds, and what can we learn by contrast about what a good shepherd will be like?
2. Read 1 Timothy 3:1–4, 8–12. What are the main differences between the qualifications for elders and those for deacons?
3. Read Genesis 3:1–7. At what point did Eve's resistance start to give way, and why?
4. Read Psalm 55. What kind of burden do you think David had in mind in verse 22?

TO THINK ABOUT AND DISCUSS

1. What qualities do you think a church might be inclined to look for in an elder if it didn't follow the Bible carefully?
2. Can you think of other examples in the Bible where one of God's people has been 'mauled' by Satan, but has then recovered?
3. Given the promises we have, why do Christians fall to temptation so regularly?

Endnotes

Chapter 1

1 Iain H. Murray, *D. Martyn Lloyd-Jones: The First Forty Years 1899–1939* (Edinburgh: Banner of Truth, 1982), p. 24.

Chapter 2

1 Henry Francis Lyte (1793–1847), 'Abide With Me'.

2 John Newton, 'Glorious Things of Thee Are Spoken', 1779.

3 C. S. Lewis, *The Last Battle* (London: HarperCollins, 1998), p. 171.

4 William Blake (1757–1827), 'Auguries of Innocence'.

5 George Richmond, in a letter to Samuel Palmer, cited in 'William Blake', Wikipedia (last modified 13 April 2016), https://en.wikipedia.org/wiki/William_Blake#cite_note-58, accessed 18 April 2016.

6 Quoted by Dr S. Lewis Johnson, Jr., 'Salvation: What Is It and Why Is It So Important?', SLJ Institute, http://sljinstitute.net, accessed May 2014.

Chapter 3

1 John Bunyan, *The Pilgrim's Progress,* Part 1, Second Stage (Logos Bible Software [n.d.]).

2 The Greek word behind 'vain ways' can be used to refer to idols—see Acts 14:15.

Chapter 4

1 See the ESV footnote to John 3:3.

2 Although not all commentators agree, I am convinced that the whole context here indicates that Peter is thinking about conversion.

3 The Greek word for 'purified' here is the one used to describe ritual purity—see John 11:55; Acts 21:24, 26; 24:18.

4 I am using the term 'brethren' here to cover both brothers and sisters. See ESV Preface regarding translation style of 'gender language'.

Chapter 5

1 Peter is here quoting the Septuagint (or LXX, the Greek translation of the Old Testament generally used at the time). The

original Hebrew of Isaiah 28:16 says that 'whoever believes will not be in haste', meaning that they will not have to flee because of having been let down by the one they were trusting in. Thus understood, the two readings, which at first look very different, are roughly equivalent.

2 See the previous note regarding the Septuagint.

3 'Incommunicable attributes' are those attributes of God that, by definition, human beings cannot share.

4 'Communicable attributes' are those attributes of God that can, albeit in a small and imperfect way, be shared with and seen in human beings.

5 Paul Gilbert, cited in *Our Daily Bread*, 16 October 1995.

Chapter 6

1 The Greek word literally means 'nearby dwelling' and came to denote anyone living in a foreign country.

2 From the song 'This World Is Not My Home' by A. E. Brumley © 1965.

3 Monasticism was a big mistake, biblically speaking. We are supposed to be salt and light; in the world but not of it. The Bible never advocates withdrawal and isolation.

Chapter 8

1 From *The Confessions of Saint Augustine*, cited in David R. Helm, *1 & 2 Peter and Jude: Sharing Christ's Sufferings* (Preaching the Word; [Kindle edn] Wheaton, IL: Crossway, 2008), ch. 11.

2 Consistency demands that if you want to argue that Peter is outlawing hair-braiding and gold jewellery, he is also prohibiting the 'putting on of apparel' according to the Greek.

Chapter 9

1 Stuart Townend, 'All My Days' (Thankyou Music, 1998).

2 Alternatively, it is possible that Peter is referring to a proclamation that the Saviour

made subsequent to his death on the cross that Scripture tells us nothing further about.

3 The term 'type' is usually used to describe an event, person or object in the Old Testament which intentionally represents, in some way, New Testament truth.

Chapter 10

1 Ella Wheeler Wilcox (1850–1919), 'Gethsemane'.

2 Cited at 'Jesus, Our Stunt Double', at Preaching Today, http://www.preachingtoday.com/illustrations/1997/december/4915.html.

Chapter 11

1 From the account in John Foxe's *Book of Martyrs*; available at John Foxe, 'The Martyrdom of Nicholas Ridley and Hugh Latimer', Theology Network, www.theologynetwork.org.

Chapter 12

1 It is important to note that, in the New Testament, two offices are referred to using three terms. There are elders/overseers (the interchangeability of the two names can be seen by comparing the terms used in Acts 20:17, 28) and deacons.

Further resources

Adams, Jay E., *Trust and Obey: A Practical Commentary on First Peter* (Wakeman Great Reprints; London: Wakeman Trust, 2000)

Bentley, Michael, *Living for Christ in a Pagan World: 1 & 2 Peter Simply Explained* (Welwyn Commentary; Darlington: Evangelical Press, 1990)

Clowney, Edmund, *The Message of 1 Peter* (2nd edn; Bible Speaks Today; Nottingham: IVP, 1994)

Grudem, Wayne, *1 Peter* (Tyndale Commentary; Nottingham: IVP, 2009)

Helm, David R., *1 & 2 Peter and Jude: Sharing Christ's Sufferings* (Preaching the Word; Wheaton, IL: Crossway, 2008)